S0-CAA-801

THE
WRECK
OF THE
OLD 97

$3.00

THE
WRECK
OF THE
OLD 97

LARRY G. AARON

Charleston   London

THE
History
PRESS

Published by The History Press
Charleston, SC 29403
www.historypress.net

Copyright © 2010 by Larry G. Aaron
All rights reserved

Back cover illustration courtesy of Gray's Watercolors of New Jersey.

First published 2010
Second printing 2010
Third printing 2011
Fourth printing 2012
Fifth printing 2012
Sixth printing 2013

Manufactured in the United States

ISBN 978.1.59629.876.7

Library of Congress Cataloging-in-Publication Data

Aaron, Larry G.
The wreck of the Old 97 / Larry G. Aaron.
p. cm.
Includes bibliographical references.
ISBN 978-1-59629-876-7
1. Railroad accidents--Virginia. I. Title.
HE1780.5.V8A17 2010
363.12'209755666--dc22
2010024367

Notice: The information in this book is true and complete to the best of our knowledge. It is offered without guarantee on the part of the author or The History Press. The author and The History Press disclaim all liability in connection with the use of this book.

All rights reserved. No part of this book may be reproduced or transmitted in any form whatsoever without prior written permission from the publisher except in the case of brief quotations embodied in critical articles and reviews.

To the memory of my late uncle J. Ryland Groff, locomotive engineer, Seaboard Air Line Railway.

CONTENTS

FOREWORD

The wreck of the Old 97 on the Southern Railway near North Danville, Virginia, on Sunday, September 27, 1903, is one of the most famous railroad wrecks in American history. From the moment of the crash until today, numerous legends surrounding this terrible event have been told and retold until it is difficult to separate fact from fiction.

Over the years, an amazing number of people have been connected to the wreck in some way—their ancestors witnessed it or arrived at the scene afterward, they were involved in the legal controversy concerning authorship of the ballad or they claim possession of an artifact from the wreckage. In other instances, they believed their ancestor was supposed to have been on the train that day but missed it for some reason.

Since researching and writing my booklet, *History of the Wreck of the Old 97*, nearly three decades ago, additional information regarding that tragic train wreck has been discovered. Dr. Larry Aaron of Danville, who shares my interest in local and railroad history, has meticulously and masterfully researched the court records of civil trials resulting from the tragedy, located and interviewed descendants of the crew and witnesses, gathered opinions from various rail experts and made logical conclusions about possible causes of the wreck.

His theory regarding the reason for the excessive speed of Old 97 as it approached Stillhouse Trestle is certainly logical. Dr. Aaron's colorful and knowledgeable commentary in this book gives the reader great insight into railroad operations in 1903 and into the role that railroads and their dedicated employees played in building this great nation.

Both historians and rail fans will gain greater understanding of the circumstances surrounding this tragedy, which occurred over one hundred years ago but continues to live on in American folklore. Dr. Aaron is to be heartily commended for his diligent research and thorough documentation of his findings.

G. Howard Gregory
Captain, Virginia State Police (Retired)

ACKNOWLEDGEMENTS

This book could not have been written without the help of a number of individuals who critiqued the manuscript, contributed photos and information, granted interviews and in other ways assisted with its publication. Because of the contributions of those below, this book contains new unpublished information related to the wreck and new photographs.

First and foremost, Howard Gregory, a retired Virginia State Police captain, published a popular history of the wreck of the Old 97 that is no longer in print. He graciously gave me permission to use his resources and also acted as consultant throughout this project.

Other authors of histories of the wreck, some just a few pages and others larger booklets, that I consulted must be acknowledged: Pat Fox, James I. Robertson, Raymond B. Carneal, Lloyd Clemmer and William Webb. Each of these writers made contributions to the story that set him apart from the others.

I could not have done without the voluminous files of information and photos of the wreck collected by Danville historian and author Clara Fountain. A retired school librarian, she authored the first children's book on the tragedy, *The Wreck of the Old 97*, which is still available.

Danville historian and friend Danny Ricketts generously shared his information about the wreck, as well as assisting me in mapping Old 97's route through Danville. He and his wife, Nancye, also published the first coloring book related to the wreck for the Old 97 Centennial celebration in 2003.

Another whose friendship I have enjoyed over the years, Lawrence McFall, provided his resources and took me to all of the local sites in Danville where one can still see the remains of the old mainline where 97 ran.

This past summer, my wife and I hitched a ride on the Western Maryland Scenic Railroad, which took us from Cumberland to Frostburg. Not only was it my first steam locomotive ride, but I also stood in the cab of a 1916 Baldwin engine, which was similar to Broady's 1903 Baldwin engine No. 1102. Special thanks to the Western Maryland management and especially to Dan Pluta, engineer and chief mechanical officer, whose photo appears in this volume.

That same weekend, I also enjoyed a ride on the Potomac Eagle, a wonderful excursion train at Wappocomo Station in Romney, West Virginia. The train was pulled by a diesel locomotive run by engineer Rodney Matheny, who also contributed to my knowledge about trains for this book.

My research was also greatly enhanced by the archives and assistance of railroad historians from the Norfolk and Western Historical Society. Thanks to Bob Cohen for his copies of train schedules and other printed materials and his general knowledge of railroad history; to Dave Stephenson, retired from the Surface Transportation Board, for his engineering calculations comparing Broady's engine with others of that day; and to Louis Newton, author and retired official of Norfolk and Western and Norfolk Southern Railways, who offered his insight into the cause of Old 97's wreck.

In addition, author and railroad historian Ed Conner, through his books and correspondence, provided information about Southern's Washington Division. Both Dr. Gene Lewis of the Greensboro chapter of the National Railway Historical Society and Dr. Frank Scheer, adjunct professor at the University of Maryland and curator of the Railway Mail Service Library, provided assistance and resources.

Other railroad men were a big help as well. They include Bob Miller of Hayes, Virginia, retired conductor for the Chesapeake and Ohio Railway; and Terry Feichtenbiner, retired engineer for the C&O, who has had extensive experience with steam locomotives. Both men gave me a great deal of insight into what might have happened in those last few moments before Old 97 jumped the trestle.

Special thanks go to a number of others who helped with specific requests: Jason Moore and Bridget Bradley of the District of Columbia Public Library, as well as Kim Zablud, Special Collections manager there; Piper Bowman, circuit court deputy clerk for Danville, Virginia, and also Trish Long from the clerk's office; Lynne Bejorneson, executive director, and Jonothan Scollo, chairman of the board, at the Danville Museum of Fine Arts and History;

Adam Goebel and Sonya Wolen of the Danville Science Center; Dr. Kenneth Ball, chairman of the Mechanical Engineering Department of Virginia Tech, along with engineering students Preston Stoakes and John Meier; the staff, especially Regina Rush, at the Small Special Collections Library at the University of Virginia; Henry Mitchell of Mitchell's Publications in Chatham, Virginia; William Gosnell of Pittsylvania County, Virginia; Carol Searcy of PIP Printers; David "Hutch" Hutcheson of Virginia MultiMedia; Alfred Scott for his senior thesis research on the authorship of the Old 97 ballad; Melissa Dabbs and Corey Furches of the City of Danville's GIS Division; Harry Haynes, manager of the Museum of the Middle Appalachians in Saltville, Virginia; and Kinny Rorrer, retired history professor at Danville Community College and old-time music authority.

A number of interviews were conducted with descendants of those who were involved in the wreck of Old 97, were eyewitnesses or otherwise had a connection in some way. My thanks to each of them for their time and contribution: Nancy Giles, William Scruggs, Danville city councilman David Luther, Howard Johnson, Bruce Clapp, Tipton Kodejs, Edwin Lawless III, Steve Maupin, Sarah Lester Adkinson, Ginger Gentry, Ann Shearer, Lankford Blanks, Fred Ingram, Henry Kritzer and Dianne McMahon.

Much appreciation goes to my former editor at The History Press, Laura All, who first assisted me with this publication. Thanks also to present publishing director Adam Ferrell, senior editor Jaime Muehl and managing editor Julie Foster for their kindness and assistance as well.

My friends Eddy and Rosanne Lloyd, along with Dudley and Bonnie Dawson (an English teacher who helped edit the manuscript), provided needed social breaks from the constant effort involved in writing this book. And my wife, Nancy, is owed appreciation for her understanding and patience as I dedicated myself to this endeavor.

In researching photo illustrations related to the wreck of Old 97 for the cover of this book, I stumbled upon one I had never seen before at Crossroads Restaurant in Gretna, Virginia, where train pictures decorate the eating rooms. Owner Fred Ingram, whose grandfather, Frank Ingram, missed his assignment on Old 97 on the day of the wreck, told me the story about how he came by the picture. A hunter was walking through the woods in the county and stumbled upon an old abandoned house, much dilapidated. On the wall, protected by a frame, was a watercolor of the wreck of the Old 97, which the hunter promptly retrieved and brought to the restaurant.

Mr. Ingram allowed me to borrow the framed print, and when I opened the back, I found a certificate with information about its origin. After a quick

Internet search, I found that the company that produced the picture was still in business. Now, this illustration proudly graces the back cover of this volume, courtesy of Gray's Watercolors in New Jersey and is available at www.grayswatercolors.com.

Finally, this volume is dedicated to my late uncle Ryland Groff, who began his railroad career as a fireman on a steam locomotive and later served as locomotive engineer for the Seaboard Air Line Railway. When I was a small boy, he lifted me up into the cab of a diesel locomotive while an engineer ran us down the track a ways. It was my first train ride and remains one of my earliest and fondest memories.

INTRODUCTION

A railroad is like a lie; you have to keep building it to make it stand.
—Mark Twain

The traditional story of the wreck of Old 97 goes something like the brief narrative you are about to read.

It was Sunday, September 27, 1903, and locomotive engineer Joseph "Steve" Broady was a man in a hurry. Fast Mail train No. 97 had arrived at Monroe, Virginia, from Washington, D.C., an hour late, and Broady was ordered to run the train, which he had never been on before, and get it to Spencer, North Carolina, on time.

Nicknamed for showman Steve Brodie, who claimed to have survived a death-defying dive off the Brooklyn Bridge, Old 97's Steve Broady was imbued with the same daredevil personality and a penchant for taking risks. Broady intended to make a name for himself, and this was his big chance.

He pushed Old 97 to the limit that day, reaching ninety miles per hour in some places, only to wreck the train on a trestle at Danville, Virginia, going much faster than he should have been. He had vowed to "put her in Spencer on time" or "put her in Hell," but he died that day with ten others, including railway postal workers on the train. Broady, so the story goes, was found with his hand still on the throttle, scalded to death by the steam.

The short chronicle of events above is a mixture of fact and fiction, and at times it is difficult to separate the two. Almost every piece of information about the story has been confused and misconstrued over the years.

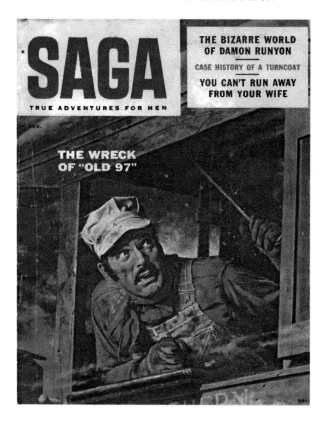

SAGA magazine featuring "The Wreck of 'Old 97'" with a caricature of Steve Broady on the cover. Hiram Herbert wrote the article in December 1956 for Mcfadden Publications of New York.

Speculation has run rampant about such things as what the engineer and fireman said to each other on the train and what Broady did or didn't do along the way from Monroe to Danville.

For example, the error still persists, even in articles in print and on the Internet, that the trestle where the wreck occurred was seventy-five feet high. Well, it wasn't nearly that high. That little fact may seem trivial, but in trying to figure out what really happened in this story, every misrepresented detail complicates the search for truth. Finding the truth behind this legend seems akin to shooting a moving target blindfolded.

That the narrative above and other published information do not necessarily represent what actually transpired in the story is not surprising. From the beginning, newspaper accounts varied, and the story of Old 97 has been enhanced again and again due to the evolving lyrics of the many versions of the famous song about the wreck. There isn't just one version of "The Wreck of the Old 97" ballad; more than a dozen exist. Yet, those endearing words have misrepresented what happened as much as anything else.

What actually happened is the topic of this book. Firsthand interviews of those who saw the wreck or were there soon after and those who observed the train along its route constitute reliable sources of information. Those who survived the wreck, plus railroad engineers and other railroad employees familiar with Broady and every aspect of railroad operations—some of whom examined the wreckage—all provide expert testimony. Furthermore, stories from the families of those who died offer some intriguing insights as well.

One of the most interesting sources of information has been the transcript from the 1905 civil trial of the Broady estate against the Southern Railway held in Danville, Virginia. Excerpts from testimony are included in the text of this book in a question-and-answer (Q&A) format. Railroad officials, surviving postal workers, local people, material evidence and statements by plaintiff and defendant attorneys shed significant light on the story and what took place.

The memories of eyewitnesses, including those postal clerks who survived the ordeal of the train plunging off the trestle, allow us to have a more defined view of the wreck. Sometimes eyewitnesses appear to contradict one another, but in seeing the event from different locations, the different versions of events often complement one another. Memories, where faulty, may result from hazy recall years later, but each makes a significant contribution to the story. From these bits and pieces, events surrounding the wreck come into focus in our minds.

The late Pat Fox, a newspaper reporter in Danville, Virginia, offered in *The Wreck of Old 97: That Most Famous Train Wreck* reasons worth repeating about why this story has attained charisma and longevity when other train wrecks have not remained in our national consciousness. Fox wrote, "But as such disasters go, it was rather a small thing. So why is it remembered at all?"

First, he suggests, there were five pictures taken on glass negatives and published in various news media around the country. Most were taken by local photographer Leon Taylor. In fact, some are seen endlessly on the Internet and often appear in books or articles written about the wreck, including this book. They capture the essence of the story.

Second, the folk ballad about the wreck became a national sensation, selling millions of records—the first song to do so. That gave the story widespread appeal.

Third, Fox reasoned, the wreck of Old 97 endures in hearts and minds because of legend. The foundation for the legend was laid with the story first reported in the *Danville Bee* the day after the wreck, September 28, 1903. Fox suggests that the reporter wrote the story on the evening of the wreck and revised it the next day. He added:

> *He probably acted as a correspondent for out-of-town papers also, as certain misconceptions and inaccuracies appear in most of the stories of the wreck published immediately following it.*
>
> *The song did not come into nationwide prominence till the 1920s. By then the facts had grown dim in the minds of men who knew it first hand. Reprinting of old errors, inconsistencies and misconceptions plus the eternally varying eye-witness accounts obscured much of the actual facts. In time even the most careful research on such a story will fail to a certain extent to separate corroborated facts from details supplied by supposition and imagination. And so the legend began and has grown continually through the years since.*

The story of the wreck of Old 97 persists and is filled with mystery, drama, questions and adventure. It takes more twists and turns than the railroad tracks on which the Old 97 ran. The story has taken on a life of its own.

What really happened on September 27, 1903, is fairly answerable and is the subject of this book. Why it happened is the real, and more difficult, question, although that, too, is worth investigating. Unfortunately, those who really know all the answers died in the wreck.

I make no claim to solving every conundrum related to the tragedy. My goal has been to shed more light on a historical event that has become an American icon.

STEAM, STEAM AND MORE STEAM

I hear the locomotives rushing and roaring,
and the shrill steel whistle.
—Walt Whitman, "Passage to India"

O ld 97, pulled by engine 1102 and others, carried the mail from Washington to Atlanta during the heyday of steam locomotives. These giant machines not only came along when the world was changing, but they also changed the world.

The steam locomotive was both a mechanical and a cultural phenomenon. Oliver Jensen, in *Railroads in America*, wrote:

> *The passage of a train closer at hand was a sight to stir the blood, as though the engine were a living thing, its exhaust panting and its great driving wheels and gleaming side rods moving in powerful rhythm. The railroad was the great mechanism of the nineteenth century and the people took it to their hearts.*

Locomotives added a new sense of adventure to life. Flanged wheels as tall as a man rolled down the mainlines of America with the haunting sounds of whistle and bell coursing through the air and coal smoke weaving, swirling and climbing to the clouds, all amid the clanking and chuffing of the engine. It was enough to charm the imagination but likely scared the wits out of anyone who had never seen one.

Deserts, mountains, canyons, prairie fires and snowdrifts were no match for these mechanized monsters. They opened up the West and created cow towns like Dodge City. They connected one end of the nation with the other. No place was far away; the world was smaller. And like Old 97, they brought the mail and newspapers across the country, illustrating that they were, besides freight and passenger haulers, a means of mass communication at a time when interstate highways, airlines and satellites did not exist.

In an era when steel mills abounded, steam locomotives were the "Gods of Iron." But despite all the romance attached to them, as the author of *The Iron Horse* wrote, "the steam locomotive with all its power to elicit emotion was just a large metal container which heated water for a fire, the resultant vapor used to drive the wheels—a most unsophisticated body." In one way of thinking, steam locomotives were just big boilers on wheels with water heated to about twice the boiling temperature, or just short of four hundred degrees, and expanded to a volume sixteen hundred times greater than its liquid form. In doing so, it gained the pressure necessary to push those big wheels down the track.

Engine 1102 was such a machine, built by Baldwin Locomotive Works, the largest builder of steam locomotives in the world. As a ten-wheeler, designated a 4-6-0, it had four lead truck or pilot wheels on the front end, six large sixty-eight-inch driving wheels under the boiler and no wheels under the cab. The four thirty-eight-inch pilot wheels were directly behind the plow-shaped cowcatcher, which was supposed to remove cows and debris from the track to prevent derailments. Of course, it didn't always work. Those pilot wheels were not attached to a power source but were allowed to swivel to help keep the driving wheels on the track, especially around curves.

The big drivers supported most of the weight of the engine, which gave the engine its adhesion to the rails. Each of these wheels also wore a metal ring, called a tire. After being heated to a high temperature, the tire was placed around the wheel and contracted to fit the wheel tightly as the metal cooled. All the wheels had flanges, which also ringed the wheel like a steel lip. On a locomotive, flanges ride up against the inside of the rails, keeping the wheels on and also suppressing the tendency for the wheels to come off the track when approaching a curve such as the trestle in Danville where Old 97 wrecked.

Steam locomotives, such as those that pulled Old 97, had the Westinghouse airbrake system. A steam pump stored air in the lines that connected all the cars, and when air in the line was released, air stored in reservoirs on each car automatically pushed against the wheel brakes to slow the train. This

Engine No. 1102, which pulled Old 97 from Monroe to Danville, is shown in passenger service in 1929 after it was rebuilt following the wreck in 1903. The locomotive was a Baldwin Class F-14, having a 4-6-0 wheel arrangement with 30,870 pounds of tractive effort. *Photo courtesy of Howard Gregory.*

was a fail-safe system, since any break in the lines resulting from an accident or other causes while the train was moving caused the train to come to a halt. With one exception. Applying the brakes too often without allowing air to build back up in the reservoirs caused the brakes to fail when they were needed. Railroaders called it "whittling," and some think that may have been the cause of the wreck of Old 97.

Overall, then, a steam locomotive was a gigantic machine, with assorted valves, gauges, rods and wheels joined together for one single purpose—to move. Yet those engines and their rolling stock were more than just a droll collection of mechanical parts hammered and bolted together. They were more than just a glorified steam engine on wheels. The fact that they were big, powerful, fast and dangerous gave them plenty of personality, too.

They propelled America from place to place in record time. Compared to horse-drawn wagons and stagecoaches, trains were the fastest things around. Those powerful engines could move a train like Old 97 down a track faster than tumbleweed in a tornado.

In 1815, stagecoaches bragged that they could travel six miles per hour between New York and Cincinnati. By the 1830s and '40s, when railroads were coming into their own, locomotives only moved an average of ten to eighteen miles per hour—fast for their day. In 1829, bystanders cheered and applauded when Stephenson's Rocket, the winner in a race between locomotives in England, crossed the finished line at twenty-nine miles per hour.

Others were appalled by those "fast" speeds. Dionysius Lardner admonished, "Rail travel at high speeds is not possible because passengers, unable to breathe, would die of asphyxia." The Bavarian College of Physicians in Germany warned, "The rapid movement [of trains] must inevitably generate in the travelers a brain disease." In *A History of Railroad Accidents, Safety Precautions, and Operating Practices*, author Robert Shaw quoted from the July 24, 1830 edition of the *Western Sun* of Vincennes, Indiana: "Twenty miles an hour, sir!...Grave, plodding citizens will be flying about like comets."

On Christmas Day 1830, the Best Friend of Charleston hauled passengers and freight over a six-mile track, becoming the nation's first regularly scheduled railway service. The *Charleston Courier* wrote in its December 29 edition: "The one hundred and forty-one persons flew on the wings of wind at the speed of fifteen to twenty-five miles per hour, annihilating time and space...leaving all the world behind."

By the time of Old 97, twenty-five miles per hour was a crawl—about the speed at which one would approach a treacherous curve, such as the one in Danville. Old 97 wasn't called a Fast Mail train for nothing. The ballad "The Wreck of the Old 97" had it "coming down the mountain making 90 miles an hour" prior to the tragic accident. An exaggeration no doubt, but it was fast.

Dave Stephenson, an industrial engineer, railroad historian and retired employee of the Surface Transportation Board, prepared statistical studies comparing engine 1102, which pulled Old 97 from Monroe to Danville, to the Chesapeake and Ohio's Allegheny and Union Pacific's Big Boy, two of the largest locomotive engines ever built. Stephenson's studies demonstrated that engine 1102 was larger than other 4-6-0 engines of its day and could easily pull twenty-five coal cars at forty miles per hour on level ground and twelve at fifteen miles per hour going up a 1 percent grade.

The most amazing results of Stephenson's calculation is that engine 1102—even with eight cars each weighing fifty tons instead of the four mail cars it actually pulled on September 27—could easily make sixty to sixty-five miles per hour on level ground. With just four cars, it would be able to run very fast uphill or downhill. The bottom line is that Joseph "Steve" Broady running Old 97 on the hilly, curvy track from Monroe to Danville could feel confident in making fast time.

Despite all the mechanical marvels associated with steam locomotives, the romance of those giants of the landscape seems here to stay. Oliver Jensen wrote, "There is more poetry in the rush of a single railroad train across the continent than in all the gory story of burning Troy." Novels, art and music have dramatized them, and railroad songs such as "The Wreck of the Old 97" have descended on the American music scene like falling leaves in autumn.

Most of all, steam locomotives and trains like Old 97 captured America's imagination early on because they seemed to be like us. Emile Zola, a French novelist, wrote in *The Human Beast*, "Somewhere in the course of manufacture, a hammer blow or a deft mechanic's hand imparts to a locomotive a soul of its own."

In *The Iron Horse*, Henry Comstock wrote:

> *Its most appealing attribute, however, was its almost human behavior. Aside from its iron belly and lungs, its pulse beat, and its highly articulate mouthings, the locomotive was a headstrong machine from the moment it was outshopped. Its behavior was well mannered or stubborn, depending in large measure upon the hand on the throttle. Again, some engines were avowed killers, while others would tear their hearts out on tasks beyond their capabilities.*

The dark side of steam locomotive travel alluded to above is what is most remembered about the Old 97 tragedy. Charles Dickens, the great English writer, illustrates it well in his description of an early train ride: "On, on, on—tears the mad dragon of an engine with its train of cars…screeching, hissing, yelling, panting."

Tragically, on September 27, 1903, Old 97's engine turned into a fuming behemoth, its firebox raging, its throat spiraling out a tornado of smoke and steam and its powerful wheels churning the air as it flew down the track with Steve Broady at the throttle. Within seconds, it morphed from servant to killer, releasing its vengeance in one last gasp.

In time, the tragedy created the ballad and story that make the wreck as vivid today as it was on that fateful day years ago. And even though steam locomotives became dinosaurs by the early 1950s, the Old 97 still rolls on.

WRECKS ON THE RAILS

Get your dinner first. There is no use your getting killed on an empty stomach.
—Yardmaster to a new switchman anxious for work

If living a life of danger and constant risk are admirable hero qualities, then the railroads of yesteryear provided plenty of opportunity for bravery and bravado. At one time, railroading was likely the most dangerous job in America, with steel mills in hot pursuit.

Besides the passengers, those who actually worked on the trains—the engineer, brakeman, fireman, conductor, flagman, postal workers and others—were most likely to be in harm's way. One old railroader said, "You only lived long enough to make one mistake." Another said, "We kill them faster than we can hire them." Those were exaggerations of course, but they bring to mind the anecdotal last verse of the song "The Wreck of the Old 97," which cautions ladies about having harsh words with their husbands, who may leave them and never return.

There weren't that many deaths and injuries in railroading until 1853 because traffic on the rails was light, trains did not run at night, speed was slow and trips were short. But railroads were built on the cheap, and they invited accidents, especially as heavier trains ran on poorly built infrastructure.

Accidents happened for every conceivable reason. Trestles wobbled, bridges collapsed, running gear and equipment such as signaling devices became faulty, boilers blew up, wheels and axles broke under pressure and shabby roadbeds became treacherous, with sharp curves and steep grades adding even more danger. And this list doesn't include a host of human errors.

The wreck of Old 97 just added names to the mounting list of casualties. The Fast Mail train was speeding through a downgrade in an effort to make up time, jumped a wooden trestle and crashed into a creek below, demolishing the wooden cars and killing or injuring most of the crew. Erupting steam and fire contributed to the macabre scene of death and destruction.

Accidents with some or all of these elements—speed, bridges and trestles, fire, escaping steam and multiple deaths—abound in railroad history. As an example, the Pacific Express belonging to the Lake Shore and Michigan Southern Railroad fell through a seventy-five-foot-high truss bridge as the train passed over it at night during near-blizzard conditions. The train with seven passenger cars crashed into frozen Ashtabula Creek, and over 90 of its 159 passengers perished. The *Chicago Tribune* for December 30, 1876, described the scene:

> *No element of horror was wanting. First, the crash of the bridge, the agonizing moments of suspense as the seven laden cars plunged down their fearful leap to the icy river-bed; then the fire, which came to devour all that had been left alive by the crash; then the water, which gurgled up from under the broken ice and offered another form of death, and, finally, the biting blast filled with snow, which froze and benumbed those who had escaped water and fire.*

This has been called the worst railroad wreck in American history. Old 97's wreck was not nearly as spectacular or as deadly as this.

Unlike the bridge failure at Ashtabula Creek, human error appears large in the wreck of Old 97, as excessive speed was deemed at fault. In a way, the wreck of Old 97 was predicted back in 1879. Charles Francis Adams, in his classic *Notes on Railroad Accidents*, wrote, "So long as trains go at great speed it is inevitable that they will occasionally be brought to a dead-stand by running upon unexpected obstacles." The trestle at Stillhouse Creek in Danville was not an unexpected obstacle, but it was an obstacle nonetheless. The result was the same.

One accident related to Old 97 that illustrates the results of speed on the rails was the wreck in 1900 of the Illinois Central No. 1 run by the famous engineer John Luther "Casey" Jones. His claim to fame comes from trying to make up time, much like Joseph "Steve" Broady attempted to do.

Wrecks on the Rails

Casey Jones, like Broady, was running a train already behind schedule. Jones and his fireman pulled out of Memphis, Tennessee, on engine No. 382 one hour and thirty-five minutes late. Canton, his destination, was 189 miles south, and Jones was determined to make up the time. The trip on the single track with traffic going both ways normally took five and a half hours at an average speed of thirty-five miles per hour. According to *Railroad Accidents* by Robert Shaw, "Specifically he would have to cover the division, including four scheduled stops, as many as 189 flag stops and an unspecified number of meets, all over a single track railroad, at an average speed of 49 miles per hour."

Casey made up time at first, but soon faced congested traffic on the southern end of his run. Casey then came into a curve, and although he was able to slow down from an estimated seventy-five miles per hour, he careened into a stalled freight train. Casey's engine and mail car suffered damage, as did the caboose and two freight cars. Casey was the only fatality.

Shaw wrote that, after an investigation, the accident report "declared unequivocally that Jones had been at fault." The investigation report noted that Casey, after he had been assigned to passenger service between Memphis and Canton sixty days before the accident, had been warned "not to attempt to establish any reputation as a fast runner and cited six previous minor accidents and several violations of the rules for which he had been held responsible."

Unlike Casey, Joseph Broady's accident with Old 97 had not been preceded by any such warning about trying to be a "fast runner." Nor was Broady cautioned because of previous accidents.

Casey's and Broady's wrecks happened within the ten-year period from 1900 to 1910, when, according to statistics presented by Shaw, fifty-eight *major* rail accidents occurred with 1,404 killed, an average of 24 per accident. Thirty-four of those fifty-eight major accidents resulted directly from human error, and nine of those were from disregarding orders.

Looking at statistics, one can see that 1903 was a significant year for railroad wrecks. Shaw includes a chart in the appendix titled "Major Steam Railroad Accidents in the United States and Canada, 1831–1977." The total fatalities for these wrecks don't include smaller incidents or those railroad accidents not associated with wrecks. The worst year was 1853, with eleven major wrecks, followed by 1912, with ten. The years 1865, 1893, 1903 and 1904 are each listed with nine major wrecks. Among these years, 1903 had the second greatest number of fatalities, totaling 204, just behind the 280 deaths in 1904

Of course, many more were killed if every accident is included. In an article published in the *New York Times* in October 1904, the paper stated, "The [Interstate Commerce] Commission began keeping statistics of fatal accidents in 1894. Since that year 78,152 persons have been killed in the United States on railroads." That ten-year period included 1903, when 9,840 were killed.

Even though train wrecks were common by 1903, the loss of eleven lives was still a sensational event, not only in Danville, with a population of seven thousand, but also around the nation. Newspapers across the region, throughout the South and in New York and Washington reported the incident.

Newspapers, of course, habitually lobotomized the railroads when serious accidents happened. Shocking, horror-filled headlines were splashed across front pages, and national journals such as *Harper's Weekly* and *Leslie's* featured gruesome sketches and descriptions. One New York newspaper editorial, reported in *Train Wrecks* by Robert Reed, noted, "The vast majority of railroad disasters are directly owing to the stupidity and neglect of the employees, and the apathy and avarice of the railroad officers."

In *Notes on Railroad Accidents* by Charles Francis Adams, published in 1879, the author laments:

> *When a railroad accident comes...it is heralded like a battle or an earthquake; it fills columns of the daily press with the largest capitals and the most harrowing details, and thus it makes a deep and lasting impression on the minds of many people. When a multitude of persons, traveling as almost every man now daily travels himself, meet death in such sudden and such awful shape, the event smites the imagination.*

Although some newspaper reports in 1903 gave graphic descriptions of the wreck of Old 97, more extraordinary events that year diminished the impact of that incident and marginalized the tragedy.

The year 1903 saw the beginning of Pepsi Cola; the New York Yankees; the Pulitzer Prizes; the first western, *The Great Train Robbery*; the premier of *The Wizard of Oz*; and the first teddy bear. More than anything else, 1903 was also a big year for transportation. Ford Motor Company produced its first Model A, and the first transcontinental trip by an automobile, and also by a motorcycle, took place that year. Columbia granted independence to Panama, and the United States purchased the assets of the bankrupt Société Civile Internationale du Canal Interocéanique, which allowed America to complete the Panama Canal.

Wrecks on the Rails

Also in 1903, Roald Amundsen left Oslo, Norway, to navigate a Northwest Passage; a new bicycle race, the Tour de France began; and the oldest speedway in the world in Wisconsin held its first race. And of course, nearly two months after the wreck of Old 97, the Wright brothers made the first sustained motorized flight at Kill Devil Hills in Kitty Hawk, North Carolina. It lasted twelve seconds—more time than it took Old 97 to leave the track, cross over the trestle that day in 1903 and careen into mud in Stillhouse Creek.

The year 1903 was part of an adventurous and reckless age, with the world growing smaller and moving faster. But Joseph Broady did not have to run the train in a reckless manner to be a symbol of his times. His was a dangerous job on a good day, as Charles Adams concluded:

> *The railroad performs a great function in modern life…and of necessity performs it in a very dangerous way. A practically irresistible force crashing through the busy hive of modern civilization at a wild rate of speed, going hither and thither, across highways and byways and along a path which is itself a thoroughfare.*

Joseph "Steve" Broady was barely in his thirties when he died in the wreck of Old 97. Had he not run the train that day, he probably would have lived out his life, and no one would have ever heard his name. As it turned out, Steve Broady the engineer has become a folk legend, and one must always wonder which fate he would have preferred.

WORKING ON THE RAILROAD

I've been working on the railroad
All the live-long day.
—American folksong, circa 1894

The engine and train crew involved in the wreck of Old 97 as it traveled the Danville Division had likely not worked together before but were cobbled together for this one specific mission: to get train 97 from Monroe to Spencer. The exception were the postal clerks, who actually were employees of the Railway Mail Service and, for the most part, were regulars on the route.

Engineer Joseph Andrew "Steve" Broady was born on April 1, 1870, to David Broady, a Confederate veteran, and Nancy Jane Carpenter. He grew up in the Tumbling Creek area of Washington County near Saltville, Virginia, during the difficult economic days following the Civil War. Whatever Joseph's experiences then, he was certainly no stranger to rugged mountain terrain, nor to railroads. Saltville had been connected by rail to Lynchburg, Virginia, since 1850.

The name Broady, pronounced "Braw-dee" by the family, reflects their Scotch-Irish origins; many Scotch-Irish immigrated to southwestern Virginia during colonial times. Like all frontier people, the Broady ancestors lived off the land and learned to survive the hard-scrabble life of the mountains. Life in the South after the Civil War could not have been prosperous for the family or anyone else in the remote sections of Virginia's Appalachian

Joseph Andrew Broady was the engineer of Old 97 when it wrecked in Danville, Virginia, on September 27, 1903. *Photo courtesy of Clara Fountain.*

Plateau. But there was coal in those hills, and developing fields needed the railroads. This brought opportunity to the area and to Joseph Broady.

Before he went to work for Southern Railway, Joseph Broady began working for the Norfolk and Western Railway (N&W) when he was about twenty-one years old. According to his application with Southern, he had served three years as a fireman and then worked nine years as an engineer for Norfolk and Western.

One source indicates that even before his work with the N&W, he may have been employed by the Seaboard Air Line Railway for a time. We have this comment from F.E. "Pete" Thompson, who was hired to Southern in 1904 and retired as conductor of train 35 on July 31, 1955. Thompson stated that he was a call boy for Seaboard Air Line Railway at Monroe,

North Carolina, and called Broady many times for runs to Raleigh. What Broady's job was is not known, nor is it for certain that he worked there.

The trial transcript from 1905 reveals that Broady's experience was known by at least two Southern employees. C.S. Lake, trainmaster of the Danville Division in charge of the traffic over the road and "in charge of employees related to transport matters," testified that Joseph Broady worked under him at Norfolk and Western. "I knew him to be a man of extraordinary qualifications; I knew that he enjoyed that reputation as a general thing."

Lake had heard through other engineers about two months before Broady was hired by Southern that Broady was anxious to come to the new employer. In fact, Lake testified that he had received a letter from Broady stating that he was anxious to come over to Southern if he could better himself. Lake further noted that he met Broady on August 3, 1903, at Franklin Junction (now Gretna, Virginia), having been sent from Greensboro by Assistant Superintendent Andrews.

Lake also indicated that he and Broady rode as far as Lynchburg together and went over conditions in general. Broady agreed to stay. Lake says that he met Broady again in Greensboro on August 5, and arrangements were made for him to learn the road. Lake stated to the court:

> *He was told when he had thoroughly familiarized himself with the physical characteristics and other conditions, to let me know and I would arrange for his mechanical exam, and would also arrange to give him a transportation rule examination. It then became my duty to examine him on the book of rules. The book of rules was gone over from beginning to end, also the special instructions in effect at that time, and we talked on general physical characteristics of the road. Broady stood a very successful examination, in all respects, and showed a striking familiarity with everything.*

Knowing the rules was not just some formality for the engineers. Running a gigantic machine with the responsibility for the lives not only of those on the train but also of those on other trains on the same tracks, as well as the safety of precious cargo, made the rules of paramount importance. Freeman Hubbard, in the *Encyclopedia of North American Railroading*, concluded, "The railroad man…had darned well better know and obey the Book of Rules, lest he find himself knocking at St. Peter's door, or at least out of a job."

Some of the rules that Lake would have questioned Broady on were those that any engineer would be responsible for, and these were brought out in the 1905 trial during the examination of Danville Division superintendent

The original application of Joseph Andrew Broady for employment with Southern Railway, used as evidence in the 1905 trial *Estate of Broady v. Southern Railway*.

E.H. Coapman. He was asked to read the following items (excerpted here for brevity) from the rule book, obviously chosen by the questioner for their possible relationship to the Old 97 wreck:

> *Rule No. 516: They must maintain, as far as practicable, regular and uniform speed…They must avoid excessive speed on downgrades and run with due caution where the track is under repair and at all points where there is reason to apprehend danger.*

> *Rule No. 519: They must make every effort consistent with the Rules and Orders and with safety to make their running time and to recover time lost.*

> *Rule No. 547: They must pay particular attention to the weather and condition of the rail, as well as the weight and speed of their trains, and give these circumstances due force in determining when to shut off steam and apply brakes, so as to make proper stops or get their trains under control.*

All engineers of the Southern Railway were expected to know and abide by these rules. In Broady's case, each rule above, and others to be mentioned later, had an impact on the wreck of Old 97.

Lake stated that he believed Broady had been an engineer about nine years and before that had worked six years as a fireman and brakeman. Because of his past experience, and having passed his mechanical and rule examinations, Broady was hired on the Southern Railway as an extra engineer. In that capacity, Broady was put on the "extra" list and would wait for assignments to come his way, although the more senior extras would receive calls first. It might have been some time before he became a regular, despite his experience at Norfolk and Western. Until the day Broady ran Old 97, his assignments at Southern were all on freight trains, no doubt comparable to his experiences at Norfolk and Western.

P.T. Bishop, who had been an engineer for five years at the Seaboard Air Line Railway, as well as at N&W, came to Southern along with Broady. The two men took examinations and learned the road together. Bishop said of Broady, "He was a good engineer…as good a one as I ever saw…I fired [meaning acted as fireman] for him several trips at N&W." He added, "He was an old runner, and when I come here [to Southern] with him, I kind of listened to him."

Joseph Andrew Broady enjoyed a good reputation as an engineer and, as far as anyone knows, did not leave Norfolk and Western under a cloud of misconduct. Also, he evidently enjoyed success as an engineer at N&W because, according to Fox's history, Broady bought the farm that he was born on and presented it to his mother and father several years before he came to Southern.

Besides being a well-respected engineer, Joseph Broady also possessed an excellent personality. Fox related, "He was tall and slim, prematurely balding, with a twinkling eye and a mouth constantly ready for a smile. He was a likeable person, kindly, not ordinarily reckless, and was much beloved

Ocie Ellen McCoy of Bluefield, West Virginia, the fiancée of Joseph A. Broady. *Photo courtesy of the Museum of the Middle Appalachians, Saltville, Virginia.*

by his family." Alfred H. Hock, a retired N&W engineer who knew Broady well, stated in an interview with Freeman Hubbard for his book *Railroad Avenue* that Broady had a pleasing personality and was well liked. Both Hock and Broady were members of the same Masonic Lodge in Bluefield, Royal Arch Chapter 20. Broady also had a girlfriend or fiancée in Bluefield named Ocie Ellen McCoy.

With such a good reputation, it appears somewhat out of character for Joseph Broady to have become known by the nickname "Steve" Broady—if, in fact, he was. As far as I know, the nickname appears only in the ballad about the wreck and is never mentioned in the 1905 trial at all. It may have been earlier in his life that Joe Broady received the moniker "Steve." On July 23, 1886, when Joseph Broady was sixteen years old, a Bowery bookie in New York named Steve Brodie caused a sensation by claiming to have jumped off the Brooklyn Bridge into the East River. He said he did it for a $200 bet.

Unlike someone who had tried the same stunt the year before and died, Steve Brodie—if he did it—survived. That he "survived" shows that it was probably a hoax, since the chances of living after a 135-foot plunge off a bridge are slim. It was reported that someone pushed a dummy off the bridge while Brodie hid under a pier close by. Brodie then swam out to a rescue boat, which picked up the "survivor."

Brodie, being a great promoter, capitalized on the event and made himself into a celebrity. He later starred in the vaudeville musicals *Mad Money* (1894) and *On the Bowery*. A Warner Brothers cartoon even showed Bugs Bunny forcing Brodie to jump off the bridge.

With all that notoriety and with names so similar, it is not hard to believe that Joseph Broady might have become "Steve" Broady.

The question is, did Joseph Broady receive the nickname because their names were similar, because he was just the opposite of the real Steve Brodie or because Joseph Broady was a reckless daredevil himself, as he has been portrayed. There is no evidence, as far as I know, to support any of these possibilities.

In an interview I conducted with the Reverend W.G. Beagle, the grandson of Broady's sister, Martha, he recalled his grandmother being very upset for a long time at the attempts to portray her brother, in story and song, as a reckless and irresponsible person. Beagle said that his grandmother told him that her brother was a very kind man and was well liked in the community. He loved the railroad and everything about it. She said that Broady was good at his job and got promoted fast. Beagle understood that Broady was not a drinker and that his family was very religious, although he offered no indication of Broady's particular faith. These comments originating with

Broady's sister are certainly consistent with comments made by co-workers and others.

Regardless of what his nickname indicated, Joseph Broady was the engineer of Old 97 on its fatal trip south from Monroe. As engineer, Broady would have had several duties. First, he was in charge of the engine, but not the train—that was the conductor's job. However, the engineer shared responsibility with the conductor for seeing that the train operated safely and that the rules and procedures of the railway were followed.

Second, as engineer, Broady not only assumed responsibility for the speed and handling of the train in transit but also the mechanical operation of the engine, especially the air brakes, which were to be tested before proceeding down the road. The engineer had to know the details of the road, the changes in elevation of the roadway, speed limits, which trains have the right of way over his train, the condition of the roadway, track geometry, signal placements, crossings, route diversions and timetable schedules involving other trains.

John Wingate, an engineer with Southern for twenty-one years, testified in the 1905 trial about additional things involved in learning the road:

> He [the locomotive engineer] *has got to learn the grades, and the curves, the trestles, the slow orders, and everything thoroughly; stations, and everything of that kind; meeting points, what points to take side track, what cross-overs, and everything of the kind about side tracks, what side of the road you go in on, and whether it is up or down grade.*

Jensen, in *Railroads in America*, noted:

> He [the engineer] *had to know a great deal about all aspects of railroading rules and signals and his job demanded that he be calm and steady in the worst situations. He had come up through the ranks, and he was doubtless hard as nails. In his day he was a figure of unparalleled grandeur.*

Jensen further added that the engineer was rarely afraid to take risks.

> His *was the judgment that determined how much a train could be pushed to make up for lost time without leaving the rails. True, the telegrapher and the conductor could "put the orders on him"—make him slow down or stop—but it was still his hand that jockeyed the locomotive.*

Working with the engineer was the fireman, who was mostly thought of as the keeper of the black diamonds and whose job it was to "shovel in a little more coal." It was a hot, dirty job, and it didn't take long to get covered in coal dust. It was said that a good fireman could shovel two tons of coal in thirty minutes.

His was an important job, but it was not so simple as throwing more coal on a fire. The fireman was also responsible for regulating the amount of water from the tender and the amount of coal in the firebox so as to maintain the needed boiler pressure for the speed of the locomotive.

With Broady on the fateful Old 97 run was fireman Albion C. "Buddy" Clapp, also age thirty-three. Clapp was born in 1870 near Whitsett in Guilford County, North Carolina, the seventh of ten children born to Alphonzo Giles Clapp and Margaret Demeris Ingle. Both of these families founded the Springwood Presbyterian Church near Gibsonville, North Carolina. Buddy was engaged at the time to Mary Stanley of Greensboro. In an interview with me, Bruce Clapp of Whitsett noted that family tradition has it that Buddy was a "wild card party man," and he thought that Broady

Fireman Albion G. "Buddy" Clapp, who died in the wreck of Old 97. *Photo adapted from the history of the wreck by Howard Gregory.*

might have been, too. However, surviving evidence seems to clear Broady of that kind of reputation.

Along with Clapp was a student fireman, John Madison Hodge, age twenty-one, from Raleigh, North Carolina. Some have concluded that he was a black man, but the phrase "black greasy fireman" in the ballad "The Wreck of the Old 97" referred to the coal dust that covered the fireman as he shoveled coal from the tender, not the color of his skin.

The conductor of train 97 was John Thomas Blair, age thirty-seven, born on March 26, 1866, near Ramseur, North Carolina. Blair began working with the railroad in 1886 and, in 1894, married Harriett Louise Bunger of Danville, Virginia. The Blair family, including their four daughters (two of them twins), were Presbyterians.

Conductor Blair would have been responsible, along with the engineer, for the safety of the train. Among his duties were communicating with yardmasters and telegraph operators regarding orders influencing the scheduled run, ensuring that rules and procedures were followed at all times and signaling the engineer when to start and stop the train.

This photo of conductor John Thomas Blair originally appeared in the *Danville Register*. Blair was buried in Danville at Green Hill Cemetery.

Flagman James Robert Moody
(February 4, 1873–September 27,
1903). He replaced regular crew
member Walter Averett Aaron on
the day of the wreck. *Photo courtesy of
Howard Gregory.*

On train 97, the flagman was James Robert Moody, age thirty, from Raleigh, North Carolina. He was born on February 24, 1873, to Albert H. Moody and Bettie Pleasants. In February 1898, Moody married Hattie Loretta Williams. The couple had three girls: Kittie Blair Moody, who died the same year she was born; Edna Van Moody; and Lois Irene Moody, born in April 1903, just five months before the wreck of train 97. Before Moody worked for Southern, he had moved from job to job. He had been a guard at the state prison, then worked at the post office and then worked for the Seaboard Air Line Railway.

As flagman, Moody was primarily responsible for protecting the rear of the train in case it was stalled or otherwise had to stop on the track. Using lanterns, flags or small explosive devices (called torpedoes, which the wheels of another train would detonate to warn the crew of impending danger), the flagman signaled other trains coming his way when his was stopped.

Moody was a substitute flagman that day on Old 97 because one of my ancestors, Walter Averett Aaron of Spencer, had been reassigned. Aaron left on train 37, which departed Monroe before Old 97 that Sunday.

Another railroader who was supposed to be on Old 97 was D. Frank Ingram. He failed to show, and the train left without him. According to Fred Ingram, owner of Crossroads Restaurant in Gretna, Virginia, and grandson of Frank Ingram, his grandfather was about twenty years old and living at a boardinghouse in Lynchburg when he was designated to travel to Monroe to board Old 97. Fred Ingram told me, "My grandmother Mary, who never ever lied about anything whatsoever, said my grandfather had had too much to drink and that's why he missed the train." Had Ingram been sober, he might have died with Broady and the others.

Clarence Goodloe was a mail clerk who was not assigned to the train but had planned to be on the train when it left Washington, D.C., that day. His grandson, Edwin B. Lawless III, shared the following with me:

> In 1903, he was a railway mail clerk, and his regular run was from Washington to Chicago escorting gold, which was being shipped to the Philippines at the time. After several runs, he would have several days off, and he would travel to Danville to see my grandmother, Sally Burton, to whom he was engaged for about eighteen years. As a railway mail clerk, Granddad was allowed to ride any train that carried mail, so on his days off he would take 97 from Washington to Danville.
>
> On [September 27, 1903], Granddad was returning to Washington from Chicago with every intention of catching 97 to Danville. His train was held up at Harrisburg due to a wreck on the main line; therefore, he was late returning to Washington and missed 97 that day. He took another train to Danville and learned later of the wreck.

Ironic though it was, one wreck saved him from another and possibly saved his life.

The postal workers assigned to train 97 were employed by the Railway Postal Service, but when they were on the train, they were under the authority of the railroad. All of the eleven postal service employees on No. 97 were from Virginia or North Carolina. The following men were still in their twenties and fairly new to the railroad: Jennings Dunlap, Percival Indermauer, John H. Thompson, Paul M. Argenbright, W. Scott Chambers, Daniel P. Flory and Napoleon Cloren Maupin. Of the others, Frank E. Brooks was the oldest, at forty-four; followed by Charles E. Reames, thirty-eight; Louis Spies, thirty-four; and John L. Thompson, thirty-six. Also assigned to train 97 was express messenger W.R. Pinckney, only eighteen.

Working on the Railroad

An article in the *Rockingham Register* of Harrisonburg, Virginia, written on October 2, 1903, a few days after the wreck, indicated that Argenbright had joined the Railway Mail Service the previous Christmas, resigning his position as principal of Keezletown Graded School. The reporter noted that the mail clerk had been in town the week before on Saturday, having been on sick leave from the railroad job, but was returning because "he was needed in the service and would have to go."

The same newspaper article mentioned mail clerk Daniel P. Flory, who had two brothers also in the mail service. Flory had been in a wreck more than a year earlier in Charlottesville in which he "received a severe nervous shock." Postal clerk John L. Thompson had also been injured in a train wreck on No. 38 in July 1903.

In an interview, Steve Maupin, grandson of another mail clerk, Napoleon Maupin, recalled fond memories of his grandfather, who related the story of his involvement in the wreck of Old 97. Steve said, "My grandfather was very intelligent, quiet, polite, refined and always wore a suit when he went to town. He was valedictorian of his high school class and could not be beaten in checkers."

Mail clerk Napoleon Cloren Maupin in his twenties. He was injured in the wreck of Old 97, but after recuperating, he continued to work for Southern Railway and later became stationmaster at Charlottesville, Virginia. *Photo courtesy of his grandson Steve Maupin of Troy, Virginia.*

Railway postal clerks spent their time sorting and bagging mail, heaving out mail sacks and snatching hanging mail bags from the upright posts at depots in order to distribute them down the line. Postmaster General Thomas L. James, quoted in *Railroading in America*, noted:

> [A railway mail clerk] *must not only be proficient in his immediate work, but he must have a general knowledge of the entire country... so that the correspondence he handles shall reach its destination at the earliest possible moment...He must know no night or day. He must be impervious to heat and cold. Rushing along at the rate of forty or fifty miles an hour, in charge of that which is sacred—the correspondence of the people—catching his meals as he may; at home only semi-occasionally, the wonder is that men competent to discharge the duties of so high a calling can be found for so small a competence, and for so uncertain a tenure.*

Keith Wheeler, in *The Railroaders*, characterizes those postal clerks as the aristocrats of the postal service, receiving extra pay for sorting mail on a moving train with the attendant excitement and opportunity of travel. If railroad postal clerks enjoyed exceptional prestige, those clerks who traveled on train 97 were an even more elite group due to their assignment on one of Southern's most important trains and its fastest train in the South.

Postal clerks endured the same privations, the same dangers and the same long hours as the engineer, fireman and conductor. In the *Science of Railroading* by Marshall Kirkman, the author elevates the postal clerk service to service in the military: "There is no distinction between a disabled soldier in the defense of his country and a railway postal servant maimed while in the performance of a dangerous duty."

Being a railway postal clerk was no mundane, nondescript job. They performed a valuable service for the nation. All together, there were seventeen men on board Old 97 leaving Monroe on that beautiful fall Sunday shortly after the turn of the century. Most were postal clerks, and for most of them—even some of the survivors—this would be their last train ride on Old 97.

SOUTHERN'S FAST MAIL

Well, look a-yonder comin'
Comin' on down the track.
—from "The Orange Blossom Special"

T he story of Southern's Fast Mail train No. 97 began way before its regular Washington–Atlanta journey. In fact, our story really begins at the end of the Civil War, even before the Southern Railway was formed.

In 1866, the Virginia legislature chartered the Lynchburg and Danville Railroad. However, according to William E. Griffin Jr. in an article on the Southern's Lima Branch, with the endeavor "coming so soon on the heels of the War Between the States, Virginia was in no financial condition to be a participant in this 'internal improvement program.'"

The Baltimore and Ohio Railroad (B&O) assumed the company stock and laid the tracks between Lynchburg and Danville. Eventually, the B&O combined the Lynchburg and Danville Railroad with its northern section, called the Orange, Alexandria and Manassas Railroad. After more name changes, it became the Virginia Midland Railway in 1881.

By 1894 the Virginia Midland had been incorporated with other lines of the Lynchburg and Danville Railway to form the Southern Railway system. As soon as Southern formed, it began a series of updates throughout the system. Raymond Carneal, in his history of the wreck of Old 97, wrote:

Immediately after the formation of the Southern in 1894, a program of improvements was begun on track structures, motive power and rolling stock…They built and opened Spencer Shops in August 1896, terminals at Monroe and Greenville, new roundhouses at Charlotte, Greenville, Knoxville and Asheville and larger shops at Atlanta.

Southern bought some of the largest passenger engines in the country, updated locomotive parts and laid new rail on the main line between Lynchburg, Danville and Alexandria in 1895. Double tracking began in Alexandria in 1902 and continued southward.

Upgrading the railway system was a top priority in lieu of the wrecks that Southern's system inherited and would continue to experience. Ed Conner, in his *Railroading on the Washington Division*, remarked that "someone looking

WASHINGTON DIVISION

Connections &
Important Operating Points

Diagram of the Washington Division showing the route of Old 97 from Washington to Monroe with important connecting points in between. *Map courtesy of E.R. Conner III.*

through newspaper files from the 1880s might get the idea that the only things that happened on the railroad—the Virginia Midland Railway, in that era—were accidents." During that time, of course, the Virginia Midland covered the territory from Washington to Danville.

According to Conner, on July 12, 1888, southbound passenger train No. 52 broke through a rickety wooden trestle at Fat Nancy Creek south of Orange (milepost 85 from Washington). The locomotive and every passenger car, except a rear sleeper car, plunged over the bridge, which had collapsed because of heavy rains. Nine people died, although the engine and train crew survived.

Conner notes that the area below Charlottesville was the scene of many railroad accidents due to rock slides and washouts. This was mainly because the tracks skirted the Blue Ridge foothills along that section, with added danger from poorly constructed curves in the track.

Even though Southern had made improvements after 1894, 1903 was among the worst years for train wrecks in Southern Railway history. As an example, on March 10, 1903, No. 39, while standing at the Danville Station, was hit head-on by passenger train No. 32, killing a passenger and a car inspector. The accident was caused by an improperly set switch.

On July 3, 1903, an open switch at the Rockfish siding caused passenger train No. 35 U.S. Fast Mail to enter the side track and collide with freight train No. 68, which was waiting there. As many as twenty-four people died, including No. 35's engineer and its fireman, the brakeman of No. 68, an engineer deadheading to Lynchburg and a boiler inspector from Atlanta. The switch was left open because the freight train conductor had misread an order and thought that the passenger train was running twenty minutes late instead of the actual hour and twenty minutes late. Carneal wrote, "The remains had to be picked up in baskets and effort made to match parts."

On July 28, during double tracking work at Springfield, Virginia, fifteen miles from Washington D.C., an unattended work train moved out onto the main line resulting in a head-on collision with passenger train No. 38, which was running late and at high speeds. No. 38's fireman, Walter Meeks, and mail clerk, W.W. Woodward, were killed, and another mail clerk, John L. Thompson, incurred a severe cut on his wrist.

Thompson worked north on No. 38, which was Southern's elite passenger train originally operated, along with its southbound running mate, as the Washington and Southwestern Limited. It later became the Crescent Limited, an all-Pullman extra-fare train that ran between New York and New Orleans. Today, Amtrak's Southern Crescent is the descendant of No. 38.

The same John Thompson was southbound as a postal clerk aboard Old 97 when it crashed, and No. 38 wound up in the first stanza of the song "The Wreck of the Old 97": "They handed him his orders in Monroe, Virginia, / Sayin' 'Steve you're way behind time. / This is not Thirty-eight, but its old Ninety-seven; / You must put 'er into Spencer on time!'"

Referring to all the accidents that happened in 1903, including many others on Southern lines not mentioned here, Raymond Carneal concluded, "There was not a man working who was not aware of the risk."

Part of the risk were the grades and curves along the tracks. The road from Lynchburg to Danville, where Broady ran Fast Mail No. 97, was not mountainous like the West Virginia route that he worked on during his time at Norfolk and Western. The elevation at Bluefield on one end of his route was 2,557 feet down to Williamson, West Virginia, at 653 feet—an elevation change of nearly 2,000 feet with all the attendant sharp curves and steep grades.

The Lynchburg-to-Danville elevation changes somewhat less, but it is still significant. *Station Directory No. 5*, dated July 1, 1912, for the Southern Railway shows that from Washington all the way to Monroe and Danville, continuous up-and-down changes in elevation took place; the lowest point was 366 feet at Fairfax and the highest was 809 feet at Whittles, a few miles from Chatham. Considering that the song "The Wreck of the Old 97" says, "It was a mighty rough road from Lynchburg to Danville," the elevation changes, plus the curving nature of the track, made the Monroe-to-Danville section the worst part of the Danville Division.

Also, when the song refers to "coming down the mountain," it is talking about White Oak Mountain having a descending grade, but that mountain has an elevation of only 1,148 feet. Once the train passed the Dry Fork station at the base of White Oak Mountain, it ran through the gap where Dry Fork creek flows between the ridges.

Moving the mail from Monroe to Danville on its route from Washington to its Atlanta destination on time was potentially hazardous on a good day. The train had to traverse a contorted terrain of tracks, interspersed with trestles, viaducts and bridges and intermingled with other connections from branch lines and trains coming directly at it on a single track. Getting the mail down the line in an uneventful way was no guarantee. Bad things could happen, as the wreck of Old 97 proved.

Worse, it was a tight schedule, and there was a stiff penalty for not getting to Atlanta on time. Fred J. Romanski tells us why in *The "Fast Mail": A History of the U.S. Railway Mail Service*:

The effect of the fast mails on the overall mail distribution system was to reduce the time in transit and promote efficiency of service, because the fast mail made connections at all important junctions serviced by the regular trains from throughout the country.

Thus, the failure to meet the Atlanta arrival time could hinder mail distribution over a wide area served by railroads coming into the city.

In volume five of *The Science of Railways*, published the year after the Old 97 wreck, Marshall Kirkman spells out the nature of the punishment for not getting the mail to its destination on time:

In the event the carrier fails at any time to transport the mail required, or fails to deliver it on schedule time at points where mail connections are made

Railway postal clerks sorting the mail. *Illustration from* The Story of American Railroads *by Stewart Holbrook, with the original appearing in* The American Railway, *1889.*

with other routes or carriers, and connections are thereby missed, a deduction proportionate to the delinquency is made by the post office department from the carrier's pay.

For transporting the mail from Washington to Atlanta, the U.S. Post Office, by an act of Congress, paid the Southern Railway $140,000 annually, an amount that would be worth about $3,500,000 today. Thus, the word "Old" in Old 97 refers not to the age of the train but was a term of endearment. It was a financial boon to the company—the pride of Southern Railway.

Because of this lucrative contract, the need for speed allowed for only a few scheduled stops for Fast Mail 97. Since it was designated a first-class train and thus had superior rights over all other trains, passenger or freight, No. 97 moved on down the line at a fast pace. Passenger trains had orders to be on a side track ten minutes before 97 came by, and freight trains were to be on a siding thirty minutes before to let train 97 pass. Nothing was meant to hold up Southern's Fast Mail train.

With the importance of the mail and baggage on board 97 on September 27, 1903, one can imagine the disappointment following the failure of 97 to meet its obligations that Sunday afternoon. Fast Mail 97 not only didn't get the mail to Atlanta on time, it didn't get the mail there at all.

LATE TO MONROE

Steve, you're way behind time.
—from "The Wreck of the Old 97"

On Sunday morning, September 27, 1903, in Monroe, a sleepy central Virginia town, nothing seemed out of the ordinary. The smoke from wood fires spiraled out of chimneys of little frame houses and rose to meet the sun as it climbed upward. It was an Indian summer day, and its warmth mingled with the quietness, only broken by church bells clanging, a sound not unlike the bells on trains arriving and departing from the depot as they head north and south.

Joseph "Steve" Broady listened for the whistle and bell of Old 97, but it was late that day, and all he heard that morning were those church bells. It would be the last time he ever heard them.

It remained a peaceful sunny morning in the town with a spirit of worship in its churches, but inside Southern's Monroe train depot things were anything but calm. The beginning of a tragedy was unfolding. The telegraph operator in Washington had sent a message to the Monroe operator that Old 97 was running late from Washington, D.C.

Old 97 had been due to leave Washington at 8:00 a.m., but trains from Philadelphia and New York arrived late that morning, keeping Old 97 in the station until all the mail cars going south were able to continue on with Old 97 or the mail was transferred to Old 97 cars. The late arrival of trains from the north would make it difficult to get the mail to Atlanta on time.

Monroe, Virginia rail yard, 1957. Old 97 left here on its fatal run to Stillhouse Trestle in Danville, Virginia. *Photo by Howard Gregory.*

When the trailing smoke of Old 97 finally appeared on the horizon at Monroe and the sound of the whistle and bell from the train echoed down the track, it was a welcome sight to Joseph Broady and his crew. They had been waiting for some time for the Fast Mail train to arrive.

In the station yard waited engine No. 1102, which had been delivered barely a month before, in August 1903, from the Philadelphia factory of Baldwin Locomotive Works. It stood ready to take train 97 on its journey southward. C.W. Elliott, foreman of the mechanical department at Monroe, testified in the 1905 civil trial of *Estate of Joseph Broady v. Southern Railway* that he inspected the engine before it left Monroe. The courtroom exchange between Southern Railway's attorney and Elliott went as follows:

> *Q. Do you remember inspecting the engine and train of No. 97 on Sunday, Sept. 27th, 1903?*
> *A. Yes, sir.*
> *Q. What kind of inspection did you make?*
> *A. We give her a thorough inspection.*

Late to Monroe

Q. In what condition was that train after that inspection, and when she left Monroe?
A. First class condition.

Before Old 97 left Monroe, engine 1102 had to build up steam pressure and change places with engine 1095, which had pulled Old 97 from Washington. That would take a little time, and there was no time to waste. Broady's watch showed that they were already an hour behind.

Ordinarily, the engineer running 97 from Washington could have made up some of the time before it got to Monroe, but when Old 97 finally left Washington, it undoubtedly ran into at least one obstacle right away—a bottleneck at the crossing of the Potomac River. Ed Conner wrote, "The old single-track Long Bridge was still in use, although a double-track replacement was being built." The *Alexandria Gazette* reported on August 26, 1903, that

> *tons of steel are arriving daily for the new Pennsylvania railroad Bridge…
> the old Long Bridge is very rickety and is the only link between Washington
> and the South…Four trunk lines of railroad use this bridge. The watchman
> at the drawbridge says that 216 trains, steam and electric, and 1700 heavy
> vehicles pass over the bridge each day.*

The bridge was so rickety, according to Conner, that part of it collapsed on October 18, 1903, about three weeks after the wreck of Old 97, under the weight of a Chesapeake and Ohio railway passenger train, killing a bridge watchman. The Chesapeake and Ohio had traffic rights on that Alexandria–Orange territory and, along with Southern trains, made that section of Southern's Washington Division the heaviest traveled.

There were also other obstacles along the track from Washington to Monroe that posed problems. On September 26, 1903, the day before 97's wreck, the *Alexandria Gazette* ran an article specifying that the double track was complete south from Alexandria (milepost 7 from Washington) to Sideburn (milepost 22) in Fairfax County and that work was progressing from Sideburn to Orange (milepost 85). In some places, the railroad had been completely rebuilt on a new right of way, and in other places, existing track was straightened out with detours for the trains during the reconstruction. There were temporary curves and conditions that would have led to slow orders that reduced speed in difficult areas.

Also, two days before Old 97 wrecked, a wreck occurred on September 25, resulting from a head-on collision at Hickory Hill (about four miles below Charlottesville) between freight trains No. 72 and 73, both trains that Broady had run in his brief time with Southern. It is possible that debris left from the wreck might still have been around and that train traffic that had backed up due to the wreck would need some time to get back on schedule.

Pat Fox, in his history, mentions that another train, halted on the track because of a mechanical problem, had to flag down 97. This incident, if true, or any of the above situations, could have canceled out any time made up by Old 97 as it headed to Monroe.

Also, regarding the double-track construction that Southern had initiated on the Alexandria–Orange section between 1901 and 1904, improving the mainline track, Conner mentions that the railroad "reduced grades and eased curves in many places" as the track made its way from Washington south, but

> on the single track south of Sideburn several troublesome segments remained. Curves abounded between Fairfax and Clifton and around Bull Run. A stiff grade against southbound traffic rose between Rapidan and Orange. A series of heavy southbound grades impeded traffic between Charlottesville and Monroe.

What exact circumstances faced Old 97's engineer as he maneuvered the train across the trestle over the Potomac River and through the maze of tracks at Alexandria, nobody knows for sure. No doubt, he headed southwest toward Monroe with the hope of making up some time. But that was not to be. Train order No. 212 was issued from Alexandria at 9:54 a.m. instructing Old 97, pulled by engine 1095, to run fifty-five minutes late from Calverton to Orange.

Whatever the reason for this run-late order and other possible delays along the way, Old 97 came down the track, skirting the Blue Ridge and passing through the hilly country around Charlottesville. It completed its 166-mile journey to Monroe outside of Lynchburg, arriving almost an hour late, without making up any time.

There to greet the late train was Broady and his crew. Joe Broady knew he needed to make up time; that's what a good engineer does—no orders needed. The bell clanged while Old 97 slowed to a halt in the train yard. Engine 1102 was at the ready, with Broady at the throttle. Fireman Buddy Clapp and student fireman Hodge manned the firebox, now red hot with coal from the tender. Broady opened the throttle, and without much delay, engine 1102 was coupled to the train. Broady checked his air brakes, whistled off and then headed south.

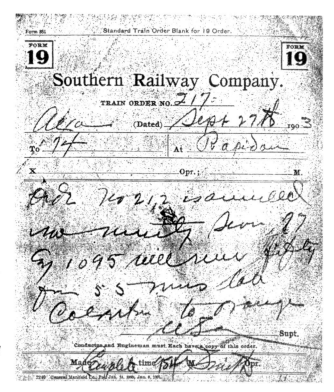

"Train Order No. 217, September 27, 1903, Alexandria to 74 at Rapidan. Order No. 212 is annulled. No. ninety-seven 97 Engine 1095 [which was pulling Old 97 from Washington to Monroe] will run fifty-five 55 minutes late Calverton to Orange. Initials of Supt. Made Complete 9:54 a.m. Smith, Operator." *Image courtesy of Howard Gregory. Translation by E.R. Conner III.*

How Joseph Broady became the engineer of Old 97 is one of the mysteries of this story and a factor that possibly contributed to the wreck. Being an extra engineer as Broady was gave him less opportunity to run a prestigious train like Old 97, but in fact, Southern was not necessarily out of line by assigning him the train. John Wingate, a twenty-one-year veteran Southern engineer, testified at the 1905 trial in response to the question, "Where are your young men, your inexperienced engineers, put to work, on freight or fast passenger trains?":

After a man has been on the road a long time, the oldest man has the preference, and they take a passenger train instead of a freight, because it is easier handled, but after a man learns the road, and the rules, and everything, he assumes the same responsibility that a man does who has been on the road 50 years…The older men have the preference but in case you want a man who has been examined and is supposed to be competent, you can put him on passenger trains, if he is available, as much as any other man.

Broady was both a veteran engineer with a good reputation who had learned the road and, evidently, in a short time, earned the trust of the Southern Railroad. Fox has suggested that

> *at the time of the wreck, railroading in the South was booming. The Southern had more business than it could handle. There wasn't enough track to take care of the traffic and fully experienced men could hardly be found to pull the trains and staff the telegraph offices. The men available were much younger and less experienced than desirable, lacking in maturity of judgment and caution.*

Fox's conclusion that Broady lacked judgment due to inexperience as an engineer in an attempt to explain his mishandling of Old 97 is not completely accurate. Certainly, Broady had plenty of experience as an engineer; he just did not have experience on engine 1102 pulling Old 97. Also, it has been stated many times in various sources that Broady did not know the road—but did he? Another question surfaces, as well: was this the first time Broady had run Old 97? The answer to both questions is yes.

Broady knew the road, its physical characteristics, crossings, warning signs and difficult areas, especially the Danville–Monroe section. A memo on Southern Railway Company stationary from the Office of the Superintendent entitled "Statement of the time by J.A. Broady, Engineer" lists every trip that he made on the payroll of Southern. The list indicates that he made the trip between Danville and Monroe twenty-two times, running freight trains. Testimony from the 1905 civil trial indicates that some of these trips were at night and others during the day.

The memo also showed that on August 30, 1903, Broady made a trip from Danville to Greensboro and back. On the sixteenth of September, he ran a freight train from Danville to Spencer and then had no assignment for ten days, until Saturday the twenty-sixth, the day before the wreck. On that day, he was aboard an Extra; that is, an unscheduled train from Spencer to Monroe. It ran the entire length of the Danville Division. The only listing for train 97 was on September 27, his last run.

Trial testimony in 1905 from W.W. Briggs, road foreman of engines, whose duty included teaching the road to new engineers, noted that he helped teach Broady. His first trip with Broady was on August 19, and he made several trips with him after that. Briggs noted that new engineers usually learn the road in ten days to two weeks. By that measure, Broady certainly can be said to have known the road well. And that may have been a reason that Broady

11—30—04. 125 M. Bezzu.   Form 719.

Southern Railway Company.

OFFICE OF SUPERINTENDENT.

STATEMENT OF TIME MADE BY J. A. BROADY, ENGINEER.

This man filed application for employment with the Southern Railway Company, August 5th, 1903, and immediately thereafter commenced learning the road between Spencer and Monroe, making his first trip on Pay August 19th, 1903.

Aug. 19th, 1903. Train 72, Danville to Monroe
    19th, 1903. Train 75, Monroe to Danville
    22d, 1903. Train 82, Danville to Monroe
    2nd, 1903. Train 71, Monroe to Danille
    5th, 1903. Train 84, Danville to Monroe
    25th, 1903. Train 71, Monroe to Danville
    27th, 1903. Train 72, Danville to Monroe
    28th, 1903. Train 83, Monroe to Danville
    30th, 1903. Train 78, Danville to Greensboro
    30th, 1903. Train 74, Greensboro to Danville

Sept. 1st, 1903. Train 72, Danville to Monroe
    1st, 1903. Train 75, Monroe to Danville
    3rd, 1903. Train 72, Danville to Monroe
    3rd, 1903. Train 75, Monroe to Danville
    5th, 1905. Train 30, Danville to Monroe (Dead head)
    5th, 1903. Train 75, Monroe to Danville
    7th, 1903. Train 84, Danville to Monroe
    7th, 1903. Train 75, Monroe to Danville
    9th, 1903. Train 82, Danville to Monroe
    10th, 1903. Train 73, Monroe to Danville
    12th, 1903. Train 74, Danville to Monroe
    13th, 1903. Train 73, Monroe to Danville
    14th, 1903. Train 82, Danville to Monroe
    15th, 1903. Train 75, Monroe to Danville
    16th, 1903. Train 75, Danville to Spencer
    26th, 1903. Train Ex. Spencer to Monroe
    27th, 1903. Train 97, Monroe to Danville

Statement from the Office of the Superintendent of Southern Railway Company listing trips made by Joseph "Steve" Broady from the beginning of his employment until the wreck on September 27, 1903. The document was used as evidence in the 1905 civil trial in Danville, Virginia.

was given the orders to run Old 97 on September 27. He knew the most difficult part of the road.

What he knew of the Danville–Spencer route is questionable since most of his training was on the Monroe–Danville track. C.S. Lake, trainmaster of the Danville Division, was asked about that at the trial. To the question, "Do you know what portions of the road he [Broady] learned?" Lake responded:

My main line territory is from Spencer to Monroe; but he gave the bulk of his time to the District between Danville and Monroe for two reasons; because that section of the road is generally conceded to be the most difficult to handle a train over, and secondly because it was intended to temporarily assign him to that section of the road.

What of the ten days at Spencer? Insight into a possible explanation came from Louis Newton, author and former Norfolk and Western and Norfolk Southern Railroad official. Newton theorizes that since Broady was a new hire and was put on the list of extra engineers, there would likely have been other engineers who were higher on that list because they had been employed longer. If the list was cut back to give the engineers with more seniority opportunity, Broady could have been sent to Spencer, where the options may have been better. Then, for whatever reason, he was sent back to Monroe.

Other perspectives have been offered on why Southern sent Broady on Old 97. For instance, Raymond Carneal, a longtime railroad man who worked as an engineer, brakeman and conductor with Southern, knew many of the railroaders working in 1903 and some who served on Old 97. His account of the wreck tells us that on September 26, engine 1102 was at Spencer and was sent north by request of Albert Dabney Shelton, newly promoted to the job of chief dispatcher for Southern in Greensboro, North Carolina.

The regular engineer of Old 97, Thomas Henry Kritzer, had been assigned to "take a diner to Greensboro creating the shortage." Joe Broady, fireman A.G. Clapp, Conductor Blair and flagman James Moody were called to take No. 1102 light to Monroe. (Student fireman Hodge is not mentioned, but he may have come on later.)

This version is consistent with an article in the *Greensboro News* on January 9, 1938. An excerpt from the article reads:

Engineer Kritzer would have been pulling "Old 97" that fateful day but for the hand of fate. C.P. Gary, known as "Parson Gary," was the regular man for the run to Spencer from Monroe. A dining car had been ordered sent south immediately on that September day and Mr. Gary ordered to go on the run. Mr. Kritzer was ordered to Monroe to pull 97 and was on his way when some trouble with the track delayed him. Engineer Broady was called and, stepping into the cab of engine 1102, he began what was to be his last trip.

Late to Monroe

An obituary for engineer Thomas Henry Kritzer appeared in the April 7, 1954 *Salisbury Post* and read, in part:

> The "Old 97" was famous even before the accident in 1903 that gave it immortality. It was a crack mail train and held to an unusually fast schedule, particularly for those days. Mr. Kritzer was one of the engineers on this train, and was scheduled to make the run the day of the accident. He was on his way south from Monroe with the train, when some track trouble at Ruffin delayed the train. As a result the crews were changed and Engineer Joe Broady was called. Broady was apparently attempting to make up the time lost by the delay because the great speed of the train was noticed by a number of persons. As a result the train went off the tracks on the trestle near Danville in one of the most spectacular accidents in Southern Railway history. Many felt that had Mr. Kritzer been at the controls the accident would not have happened.

Henry Kritzer, age eighty, of Greensboro, North Carolina, grandson of Thomas Henry Kritzer, relayed yet another version to me during an interview. When information came that Old 97 would be arriving in Monroe late, Southern decided to create a first section for Old 97 run by Kritzer. It would go ahead of the regular run coming from Washington and would keep Old 97 from being late to Atlanta. Broady's train would have been the second section. The first section would pick up mail all the way down but would not have any to drop off from Washington, which the later train could do. Engineer Kritzer's grandson said:

> What I recall he told me was that he was headed south to take some car to Greensboro. He left Monroe on time for the regular schedule for 97. Apparently, he had some mail on board so that the railroad would not be penalized for running the mail late. I believe that he expected 97 to catch up before he got to Spencer. I also believe that he told me that he picked up mail in Danville. He was in his early eighties when we had this conversation, and I was nineteen or twenty. However, I always felt that he remained mentally sharp until the last year of his life.

Supporting this second section scenario is a soiled and damaged green flag found in the wreck of Old 97. A green flag flown on the engine of a train might indicate a second section, but this flag might have been kept on the train for the flagman to use for other purposes.

This soiled and damaged green flag found in the wreckage of Old 97 may have been used as a signal device by the flagman or mounted on the engine to indicate a second section of a train. *Courtesy of Danville Museum of Fine Arts and History.*

Pat Fox added another twist to this story about a second section:

On the evening of September 26, 1903, a second section of the fast passenger train number 37 came through Monroe and the waiting 97 crew was ordered to pull her out. That left a vacancy. After receiving telegraph notice, D.B. Nolan at the Danville Division headquarters in Greensboro made up a spare crew to fill the void and deadheaded them north to Monroe aboard a freight. It was this special crew, which was waiting when Old 97 came in from Washington the next day.

My own Aaron family history indicates that Walter Aaron, who was replaced by Moody on train 97 during its fateful journey, supposedly left on train 37, which corroborates the story above. But added to that story is another. A Southern Railway memo published shortly after the wreck stated, "Walter A. Aaron was called for baggagemaster but was ask[ed] by Pollie

Hopkins from Brown Summit, N.C. not to go, get left and go with him on another train following 97 that day."

Just to complicate things a little more, an interview with W.E. "Bill" McIvor of Lynchburg appeared in the *Washington Star* Sunday magazine for November 5, 1967. In the article, McIvor claims that he tried to prevent what became the wreck of Old 97. Neal Ulevich, a journalism student at the University of Wisconsin at the time and later recipient of the Pulitzer Prize, wrote "Her [Old 97] regular crew was shifted to a charter train, and rookie engineer Joseph (Steve) Broady was picked—probably by accident—to take the steam-driven train from Monroe to Spencer, N.C."

The article continues with McIvor, who worked at the Monroe station, offering the following exchange between himself and Broady: "He walks up to me and says he wants the train. I never seen him before and I told him 'I don't believe you know enough about the road to run that train.'"

Ulevich added, "Broady had never made that trip, but became offended when challenged." Again quoting McIvor, Ulevich wrote, "It was against the rules to give him that train. He thought I was insulting him, so I [McIvor] says, 'Get permission by telegraph.'" Broady did exactly that, the story goes, and McIvor "reluctantly handed him his orders and watched Broady take over the train." It is easy to understand how McIvor would not have known Broady. Howard Gregory says, "Broady had been on the Southern for only a month and in Monroe much less than that. Monroe was a busy place with a lot of rail crews in and out."

These confusing and contradicting versions of why Broady received the assignment to run the coveted Fast Mail train have similarities that might be reconciled. Taken together, it is possible that all the stories contribute to the truth of why Broady was given Old 97.

If Broady and his crew had been assigned to Old 97 on the day before the wreck, all or some of them might have taken the Extra train to Monroe for that purpose. In that case, neither Broady nor his crew would have known ahead of time that Old 97 would be late the next morning. It is entirely possible that the Old 97's late arrival from Washington was unexpected by everyone at Monroe.

One thing is true in this story. Steve Broady had his orders, but they weren't to get the train to Spencer on time or to make up the time. In the first place, the railroad would not have ordered any man to do so. Although he was expected to make up such time as he could within limits, he did receive other orders—slow orders and run-late orders like those received by the engineer of engine 1095 pulling train 97 from Washington to Monroe.

One order, No. 725, sent from Greensboro to all trains was in effect:

> *Trains will reduce speed to six miles an hour over Cherrystone bridge* [near Chatham], *and to 20 miles per hour between 192 and 193 mileposts* [about 20 miles south of Lynchburg], *and over Otter River Bridge* [at milepost 193.6].

Even though Old 97 was delayed, other trains continued to advance up that single track toward Monroe, and that complicated matters. Because the schedule was now altered by the late train arrival, the Monroe station operator wrote out Order No. 339 instructing Old 97 to run twenty-five minutes late from Monroe to Danville. To make matters worse, before Conductor Blair of 97 saw that order, another was instituted because information from Washington indicated that Old 97 would be later than first stated. Order No. 340 came into the telegraph office at Monroe, stating: "Order No. 339 is annulled. No. 97, Engine 1102 will run 45 minutes late Monroe to Lynchburg, and 40 minutes late Lynchburg to Danville." Both orders were signed under the authority of E.H. Coapman, superintendent of Southern's Danville Division.

These orders meant that Broady could not push the train at just any rate of speed without undue consequences. Even though he left Monroe at 1:08 p.m. instead of the regular time of 12:04 p.m.—a difference of an hour and four minutes—these run-late orders meant he could only make up so much time before his arrival in Danville.

The original arrival time in Danville, if Old 97 had not been running late, would have been 1:45 p.m. The last run-late order required that Old 97 not arrive in Danville before 2:25 p.m. that Sunday afternoon. If it did, it would have to wait until 2:25 p.m. before proceeding further. Had Old 97 gone down the track unrestrained, with at least two other northbound trains on the same track, a head-on collision would have occurred, despite the fact that 97 had right of way over all other trains.

E.H. Coapman had the following exchange with a prosecuting attorney in the Danville trial:

> *Q. What was he expected to do?*
> *A. He was given an order that would not allow him to arrive at Danville until 2:25 P.M.*
> *Q. Wasn't he to do his best to get in here at 2:25, if he could?*
> *A. He couldn't do it.*
> *Q. Wasn't he to do his best?*

Cap. of Siding in Cars.	Miles from Washington.	Time Table No. 8. In Effect Mar. 26, 1899. STATIONS.	Sta'n Nos.	Min'm Time bet. Stations Frt. Trains.
		Lv. Ar.		
150	166.1	.........Monroe.........N	166	
		1.5		8
33	167.6	.......Burfords........D	168	
		4.3		9
19	171.9	.....Island Switch.....	....	
		0.2		½
....	172.1	C. & O. Crossing..N	172	
		0.8		2
....	....	..N. & W. Crossing..	....	
				....
348	172.9	W......Lynchburg.....N	173	
		1.8		4
32	174.7	............Caseys	175	
		1.5		3
....	176.2	.........Durmid.........	176	
		0.9		2
66	177.1	............Wilmer........N	177	
		1.4		3
35	178.5	........Lucado...........	179	
		5.2		10½
92	183.7	W..Lawyer's Road..N	184	
		6.0		12
43	189.7	.........Evington ......D	190	
		2.2		4½
14	191.9	...........Davis.............	192	
		1.7		3½
120	193.6	.......Otter River......	194	
		2.4		5
80	196.0	.........Lynch's........D	196	
		3.7		7½
84	199.7	W...........Hurt...........N	200	
		3.7		7½
67	203.4	.........Motleys...........	203	
		3.0		6
40	206.4	.........Sycamore......D	206	
		4.0		8
21	210.4	.....Ward Springs......	210	
		1.0		2
178	211.4	W..Franklin Junc...N	211	
		3.4		7
39	214.8	.........Galveston.........	215	
		1.6		3½
85	216.4	.........Whittles ......D	216	
		4.8		10
100	221.2	W ....Chatham........N	221	
		4.9		10
51	226.1	.........Dry Fork..........	226	
		5.2		10½
103	231.3	.......Fall Creek.......N	231	
		2.7		6
45	234.0	.............Lima.........	....	
		3.9		8
134	237.9	....North Danville....	238	
		0.8		
626	238.2	W......Neapolis ....N	....	
		Ar. Lv.		

"W," Water Station.
"D," Day Telegraph Station.
"N," Night and Day Telegraph Station.

An 1899 Southern Railway Employee's Timetable listing the stations between Monroe and Danville, Virginia, including miles between stations and miles from Washington, D.C. *Illustration courtesy of Howard Gregory.*

A. When we have a late train, as I explained, we give them an order to run so many minutes late, which sets their schedule back so many minutes for that date and that train, allowing opposing trains so many more minutes to make advance stations.

Running an hour behind schedule, it was possible for Broady to make up about twenty minutes of the time, arriving at Danville exactly forty minutes late as instructed, instead of one hour late. Coapman gave the following testimony in an exchange with the plaintiff's attorney:

I have tried to explain to you that No. 97 of that day, or No. 97 of any other day, or any other train of any other day, that is running an hour late, by actual time receives an order to run 40 minutes late, if their schedule is so that they can make up 20 minutes, very good, but the engineer is not ordered absolutely to make up that time. In other words, he is allowed to make up what time he possibly can, his judgment and the conditions being taken into consideration.

Coapman continued, "We leave the running of the train, so far as speed is concerned, entirely to the judgment of the engineer, for the reason that we cannot reach the engineer between stations." So Southern did not order Broady to make up time but would have allowed him to make up some twenty minutes depending on his judgment and would have been happy if he did so.

Not only was Broady confronted with slow orders for bridge repairs and run-late orders, but he also had a scheduled stop at Lynchburg, a short distance from Monroe. Broady might have considered that if he could arrive in Danville forty minutes off schedule instead of one hour, then perhaps he could make up the rest of the time on the way to Spencer, a line without the hills and dales he was facing toward Danville. With all the obstacles he faced, averaging fifty-five miles an hour to Spencer would have been difficult and necessitated pushing the train much more than that speed when possible.

The testimony of Superintendent Coapman was that the regular run of Old 97 between Lynchburg and Danville required Old 97 to do the sixty-six miles in eighty-five minutes, which he agreed was forty-eight miles per hour under normal conditions. If, as asserted in the trial, Broady had twenty-eight minutes to make up between Lynchburg and Danville, he would have had to run an *average* of sixty-eight miles per hour, meaning even faster in some places. Coapman testified that he would not have been able to make up that time.

Late to Monroe

Joseph "Steve" Broady—poised at Monroe on Old 97, likely having arrived the day before, destined to travel a familiar route even though it was a train he had never been on before—prepared unknowingly for the ride of a lifetime. Finding out that the train would be late and presented with the challenge of making up a great deal of time because the Washington Division crew had not done so, Broady must have been frustrated as he faced one obstacle after another. Perhaps the biggest challenge of all was one noted by Dave Stephenson, "It's likely that the schedule for a mail train was set very tight, not much slack built in, and average speeds fairly high. Therefore, there would be little opportunity to make up time except by going as fast as possible."

In an interview previously mentioned, Joseph "Steve" Broady's sister, Martha, told her grandson, the Reverend W.G. Beagle, that her brother was "a perfectionist and very big on being on time [in his railroad job]." Whether that led to him being in a hurry to the point of recklessness is still debatable, though it is doubtful considering the type of person he was reported to have been. Even so, making up the time that day wasn't going to happen—not then, not ever.

RUNNING LIKE THE WIND

When we cross that White Oak Mountain
You can watch Old 97 roll.
—from "The Wreck of the Old 97"

With side rods glistening in the sunlight as they moved in horizontal rhythm, rotating forward and backward, smoke and steam streaming upward in a spiral from the cylinder stack, the engine picked up speed. Slowly at first, the train moved forward with a long pause between the chuffing sounds generated by steam release. The pauses got shorter as Old 97 picked up speed and the big driving wheels brought the iron horse to a gallop.

Although locomotive 1102 and its tender pulled Old 97, the train of cars behind it was the important thing. The train makeup was as follows: the engine (which was not always engine No. 1102) and tender, two postal cars, an express car and the baggage car. In an interview with the *Virginia Star* of Culpepper, published on August 10, 1933, mail clerk Charles. E. Reames related that the express car was right behind the engine tender, followed by the head postal car, the mail storage or baggage car and, finally, the rear postal car.

L.W. Spies, Charles E. Reames, Dan Flory and N.C. Maupin, with substitutes Argenbright and Indermauer, worked on Fast Mail 97 in the postal car right behind the express. In the last postal car were John Thompson, mail clerk in charge; Frank Brooks; J.J. Dunlap; J.L. Thompson; and Scott Chambers. These mail clerks running out of Washington were due to be relieved in Greensboro by clerks from Atlanta.

Baggage cars held still more mail in pouches and sacks, sometimes human remains and also passenger luggage, which it did not carry on Old 97. The express car held freight, some of it in wooden crates. A safe was also aboard this car. The contents were in the custody of an express messenger of the Southern Express Company.

With Joe Broady's hand on the throttle of the engine and the postal cars trailing behind, Old 97 pulled out of the Monroe station at 1:08 p.m., an hour and four minutes late. By orders, the train could not arrive in Danville earlier than forty minutes late, which meant that Broady could, at most, make up twenty-eight minutes by the time he got to Danville.

Armed with run-late orders because other trains were on the single track heading northward and slow orders due to bridge repairs and track conditions, Broady certainly must have realized that making up the total time he needed by Spencer would be difficult. Plus, he had to stop in Lynchburg, then Danville and later Greensboro. How much effort he put

Engineer Dan Pluta of the Western Maryland Scenic Railroad in a 1916 Baldwin 2-8-0, imitating Steve Broady with one hand on the whistle and the other on the throttle.

into getting to Spencer on time is a major question, but his desire to make up some time would have been normal for any engineer when his train was behind schedule.

Lynchburg, 6.8 miles south of Monroe, was the next stop. That stop, too, became a problem. Trial testimony indicates that there was some delay at Lynchburg in unloading the Sunday papers.

But Broady was also confronted with two more orders at Lynchburg. At 1:20 p.m., Conductor Blair of Old 97 signed order No. 341, which had been sent to Lynchburg station at 1:12 p.m., while Old 97 was between stations. The new order read, "No. 97, engine 1102 will meet No. 36, engine 1073, at Whittles, and No. 30, engine 1088, at Fall Creek." At 1:21 p.m., while 97 was stopped in Lynchburg, Conductor Blair received order No. 342 changing the previous one. It read, "No. 97, engine 1102 will meet No. 36, engine 1073, at Chatham, instead of at Whittles. E.H.C."

Not only did that change things but something else also developed, of which Broady likely had no knowledge. Southern Express Company had employed Wentworth Armistead as a safe locker since the previous December. His job was to lock the safe after all valuables had been loaded. Entrusting only station employees with the safe's combination protected against possible train robbery. However, after locking the safe, Armistead was supposed to get off, but Old 97 left with him still aboard.

Howard Gregory offers a couple reasons for why this may have happened. Both Broady and Blair may have been unfamiliar with the procedures at the Lynchburg Station, and both the engineer and the conductor were aware of the need to make up lost time. It is also possible, suggested Pat Fox, that Broady could have misunderstood a sign from Blair to hold the train or he just chose to ignore it.

Either way, the train started moving with Armistead aboard. Perhaps Armistead could have scrambled off, but he didn't. He probably planned, as Gregory suggests, to return on a northbound train later in the evening when it departed from Danville. Regardless of his decision, the train ride would be his last.

In the confusion after the wreck, it was also reported that Ralph Thompson, the twelve-year-old son of postal clerk John L. Thompson, was on the train. If so, his presence would have absolutely been against railroad policy. He supposedly boarded 97 in Washington and came with his father down the line. Instead of getting off in Lynchburg to visit relatives, he continued on and was allegedly killed in the wreck. However, his body was never found, and there is no indication that he was ever on the train.

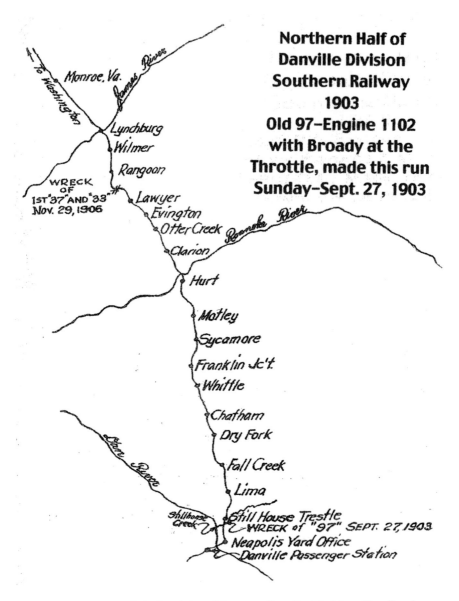

Northern Half of
Danville Division
Southern Railway
1903
Old 97–Engine 1102
with Broady at the
Throttle, made this run
Sunday–Sept. 27, 1903

The mainline route that Old 97 took from Monroe to Danville, Virginia, with railroad stations indicated, along with Stillhouse Trestle. Samuel Spencer, the first president of Southern Railway, lost his life near Lynchburg in the wreck between No. 37 and No. 33 in 1906. *Adapted from* Wreck of Old 97 *by Lloyd Clemmer.*

Running Like the Wind

As Old 97 pulled out of Lynchburg and sped southward, it rolled through crossings at Lawyer's Road, Evington, Otter River and Lynch's Station and then across the Staunton River Bridge into Pittsylvania County. It hurled steam and smoke along its path toward Hurt, Motley and Sycamore, all only a few miles from one another. Ten miles south of Staunton River Bridge lay the community of Franklin Junction, or Elba, both names for present-day Gretna.

Old 97 might have stopped for water if needed at Gretna, but on that Sunday afternoon it flew by the station in a cloud of dust. On May 7, 1933, the *Richmond Times-Dispatch* published an interview with David Graves George, a Southern Railroad employee at the Gretna station who came to national attention as author of the song "The Wreck of the Old 97." George gave his version of the train's arrival at Gretna, ten miles from Chatham:

> *Marvin and me were standing there when we saw that train coming. He had her wide open; he was a new engineer and they told him to be sure and put 'er into Spencer on time. There was a little curve in the tracks and Marvin and me thought he was going to bust right through the depot there.*

Railroad depot at Franklin Junction, now Gretna, Virginia. Notice the water tank on the right. Old 97 did not stop in Gretna the day of the wreck to take on water as was previously thought. *Courtesy of Fred Ingram of Gretna, Virginia.*

We ran back out of the way, but she rocked around the curve. Look at that damn fool go, Marvin said.

In another interview with the *Detroit Free Press*, George recalled:

There was a steep grade just out of town, and when they came up they always had to stop for coal and water... Well on this particular day, he [the engineer] came highballin' through there with a full head of steam, and never so much as whistled. I even had to jump back to get out of the way. The track supervisor [Marvin Murphy] said he guessed something was wrong and I said I guessed as how that was.

After passing through Gretna, Old 97 rolled by Whittles and, four miles down the road, past Chatham. Pat Fox expressed it this way:

Ninety-seven roared through Chatham, her bell ringing and leaving a cloud of dust behind her a mile or more along the track. People rushed from their houses but did not see the train. They saw only the cinders, smoke and dust. And they heard her mournful whistling as she charged on toward Dry Fork and White Oak Mountain.

Train No. 36 waited on a side track at Chatham, giving Old 97 the right of way before the northbound train advanced, itself leaving Chatham seventeen minutes later than usual.

Dry Fork, at the base of the mountain, lies five miles below Chatham. Old 97 did not slow down for the mail at that station. As the train maintained high speed while approaching the mountain pass, it swayed and lurched along the track, pulling up roadbed dust. Mail clerks threw off a bag of mail but were unable to use the extended arm of the mail catcher to grab the mail pouch hanging from the suspension arm at the Dry Fork depot.

The grade up White Oak Mountain involves an elevation change of less than 2.0 percent, so the mountain climb is not up high peaks on switchback curves with struggling upgrades and steep descents. It has been established that with a locomotive like No. 1102 and only four trailing cars, the train could easily ascend the grade at sixty miles per hour without a problem. As mountains go, White Oak Mountain is more of a hill. In addition, the mainline went between the peaks. As previously noted, a 1.5 to 2.0 percent grade is significant for a train, but Old 97 certainly wasn't huffing and puffing its way to the top.

The Dry Fork Depot at the base of White Oak Mountain. Old 97 sped by the station so fast that mail clerks were unable to use the train's mail catcher arm to grab the suspended mail pouch hanging outside the station. *Photo courtesy of Howard Gregory.*

As Old 97 descended the mountain, it naturally would have picked up speed as it made the three-mile descent to Fall Creek. John H. Groff, my great-great-grandfather, a Swiss immigrant who farmed near the tracks coming down the mountain, commented that "Old 97 was really rolling."

Ed Williams, who resided in the Witt community, had a blacksmith shop at nearby Fall Creek station. He often repeated the story that while standing near the tracks as Old 97 passed, he "was almost pulled underneath the train due to its excessive speed as engineer Joe Broady thundered by."

By the time Broady reached Fall Creek, less than ten miles from Danville, one would think that he would have gained a good deal of time. However, trial testimony from Danville Division superintendent E.H. Coapman stated otherwise. The following statement was recorded on July 11, 1905:

> *We have engineers who have made the time between Monroe and Danville in much quicker time than that. That run of No. 97 of Sept 27th is hardly up to the average runs of 97 since it has been on the time table.*

Coapman revealed even more under continued questioning:

> *Q. It [Old 97] left Monroe at 1:08 and passed Fall Creek at 2:36.*
> *A. That is one hour and 28 minutes; their running time you say is what?*
> *Q. According to the schedule, from 12:04 to 1:34.*

Fall Creek Depot at Witt, Virginia, in the early 1970s. Old 97 rushed by this station only minutes before it crashed at Stillhouse Trestle. The station was later converted into the Old 97 Steakhouse. *Photo courtesy of Howard Gregory.*

A. That is one hour and 30 minutes.
Q. It made up two minutes and only two minutes. I ask you if that is an appreciable quickening of speed.
A. No, sir, it is not.

Despite the anxiety over Old 97's lateness, by that time of day it was a forgone conclusion among Danville folk that the train was seriously off schedule. Having gained only two minutes by the time he arrived at Fall Creek, Broady had to have realized that he had only made up a little lost time.

From Fall Creek to Lima is about four miles and includes a substantial elevation change upward. But with 97's capability, the transit would not have sapped the momentum gained from its downhill descent as much as one would think. From Lima onward, the trip from Lynchburg was open throttle all the way to Danville.

How fast was Old 97 really going from Lynchburg to Danville? The only ones who could really testify about the ride from Lynchburg were surviving postal clerks, and some did so in the 1905 trial. Postal clerk N.C. Maupin, who was in the second car behind the engine, was examined in court about his impression of the speed of the train from Lynchburg to Danville. His testimony in that regard stated that at the time of the crash he thought the train was running fifty to sixty miles an hour. Then followed further questions and comments:

> *Q. Had it run that fast all the way from Lynchburg?*
> *A. Not in all places, I don't reckon.*
> *Q. You agree then that it didn't check up from Lynchburg to Danville?*
> *A. I never noticed particularly along there.*
> *Q. What was the usual rate of speed on 97?*
> *A. Some places faster than others.*
> *Q. You paid no particular attention to the speed of the train until this accident caused you to remember the speed on that particular day, did you?*
> *A. I remember one place it was running real fast.*
> *Q. Where was that?*
> *A. Elba.*
> *Q. Between Danville and Lynchburg?*
> *A. Yes.*
> *Q. Was it running all the way from Lynchburg to Danville very rapidly?*
> *A. No, just that one place.*

Charles E. Reames, who had been a postal clerk since 1895, testified that Broady did not slow down or "check up" from the time he left Lynchburg. "I suppose he made an average speed of about 45 miles an hour." He stated to the court that he had timed trains before and had an idea of how fast they were running.

The attorney and witness went through an extensive and interesting exchange, excerpted below:

> *Q. Do you know when you passed Elba?*
> *A. I do.*
> *Q. Running very rapidly there?*
> *A. I thought he was going to break the car in two, going around that curve.*
> *Q. You know whether they were running so very rapidly at Elba, and you know whether Broady was running so very fast prior to this, but you don't know whether he was running fast, as a rule, from Lynchburg to Danville?*
> *A. Yes, the train runs fast all the time, but he never slowed up anywhere.*

Q. Was it running unusually fast that day?

A. On some parts of the road he was not.

Q. Specify those parts.

A. From Lynchburg up to Lawyer's Road he was not running unusually fast.

Q. Was he running unusually slow?

A. No.

Q. When he was running from Lynchburg to Lawyer's Road, was he running much slower or faster than the usual rate of speed?

A. I suppose about the average rate of speed.

Q. Where else did he run slow, or about his usual rate of speed?

A. From Otter River up to Lynches.

Q. Was he running about his usual rate of speed again?

A. Yes.

Q. Where did he run at an unusual rate of speed, except at Elba and prior to getting to the trestle?

A. Running around those curves just before he got to Staunton River.

Q. How did he run from Staunton River to Chatham?

A. From Staunton River to Chatham is all uphill.

Q. Did he make the usual, or a slower rate of speed?

A. I suppose he kept about the usual rate of speed.

Q. Was the average rate of speed from Lynchburg to Danville much greater, or much less, or about the same as the regular schedule rate?

A. I don't suppose it was much more than the regular schedule.

Q. Then the regular schedule made him run like the wind, didn't it?

A. The schedule is fast.

Q. You think there was very little difference in his general run from Lynchburg to Danville that day?

A. I don't think there was much difference, take the general run, all the way through.

Q. Then the general run, all the way through, had to be made at a high rate of speed?

A. Yes, sir, the general run has to be made at a high rate of speed.

Regardless of how fast the train was running from Lynchburg to Danville, it was at Lima that things changed. From there, everything went downhill, literally and figuratively. But no one in Danville was aware of it at the moment. People were going about their normal Sunday afternoon business: attending church, enjoying Sunday dinner or resting and relaxing. It was not a cloudy day; the only cloud was the stream of heavy dark smoke forming a ribbon behind Old 97 as it thundered down the last stretch of track toward Danville.

Among those unaware of impending disaster was twenty-two-year-old E.H. Chappell of Harrison Street, near the Betsy Rice Cut at Third Avenue. He was taking an afternoon nap. So was Mark Daniel Jones, the grandfather of local historian Danny Ricketts. That afternoon, too, Daisy Willis and her family were enjoying a late Sunday dinner at their home near the trestle. Mrs. B.S. Hundley and her brother were standing on her porch trying to get relief from the eighty-degree temperature. L.C. Jordan, who had moved to Danville in August 1903 and rented on Farrar Street, was walking in his backyard.

Nineteen-year-old Oscar Hardy was at church with his family on nearby Keen Street during the two o'clock hour. Everyone walked to church, so services were held in the afternoon. At Will Payne's church, he was standing on the front porch catching some fresh air while the congregation suffered from the heat and the intense message about a world full of sin about to be destroyed.

Ruel Bullington, a youngster of six, and his family had moved from Swansonville to Danville two years earlier. In the summer of 1903, they had moved to Washington Street on the north side of the Dan River and resided in a home on the hillside not far from Stillhouse Trestle. Bullington, who later retired from Danville Knitting Mills, stated, "To us, just watching a train was something special." So it was on that Sunday, September 27, that he and his older brothers went down near the trestle after Sunday dinner to watch the trains round the bend.

With Old 97 less than five minutes away, two small children were playing under the trestle, while George Broady waited at the Danville Station for his brother, engineer Joe Broady, with a letter from their mom.

Other folks were waiting anxiously, as well. John Lindsey Moore had moved from North Carolina to Danville and at the time was an apprentice mechanic; later in life, he became superintendent of Danville Knitting Mills. He and other gentlemen were sitting on the porch at a boardinghouse on nearby Worsham Street waiting for the train.

Herman Lester had come in from the country to visit his cousin James Lester. James worked as a clerk in the retail grocery store and wood yard of J.R. Hodges on the corner of Henry and Claiborne Streets in Danville. Part of his job on Sunday was to meet "the colored drivers at the stables… to feed and water the dray horses." By the time Old 97 approached, he and Herman were nearing the crossing on Henry Street.

As Old 97 reached Lima, sixteen-year-old John Wiley, who worked in Riverside Cotton Mill's cloth storage building next to the trestle, was walking with a girlfriend along the grassy knoll on Reservoir Hill, which overlooked the trestle.

Local historian Lawrence McFall wrote about his grandfather Earl Nostrandt's experience that day. Earl's father was a loom fixer in one of the mill buildings near the trestle, but on that Sunday, Earl's family had left the Presbyterian church on North Main Street and walked home to their house on Myrtle Avenue. There, Earl joined his friends Robert Harris and Ned Williams in shooting marbles in a ring cut in the red clay dirt in Earl's front yard.

It was only moments before Old 97's whistle would echo in the ears of those near the trestle and they would take notice of a tragic event—one that would change their lives and the history of Danville, as well as railroad and music history. When their ears perked up and they heard the screaming whistle, they could not have known that when they got to the trestle minutes later, they would be hearing the screams of the wounded and dying.

THAT THREE-MILE GRADE

He was going down grade making 90 miles an hour,
When his whistle broke into a scream.
—from "The Wreck of the Old 97"

At Lima began a three-mile grade to the wreck site of Old 97—five minutes or so running time. Worst of all, it was all downhill. If Broady had indeed bragged that he would get Old 97 to Spencer on time or to hell, his prediction was about to come true. By the time he reached Fall Creek Station, a few minutes outside of Danville, he had made up only about two minutes of time, and it was still quite some distance to Spencer. But hell was coming up—in the form Stillhouse Trestle.

No one knows what conversations took place in the cab between the firemen and the engineer or what decisions were made during those last few minutes regarding the speeding train. Was Broady on a suicide mission? No engineer who knew Broady or worked on the railroad believed that Broady had a death wish and deliberately rode Old 97 down the three-mile grade from Lima intent on wrecking the train. While we don't know everything about Broady's personality, and no one knows exactly what was said in those last moments, we do know one thing: Broady had to know the trestle was coming up.

It is difficult to believe that Broady didn't recognize the terrain and sites that indicated he was approaching the trestle. He had been over the road enough to recognize landmarks, and he knew how dangerous the curve

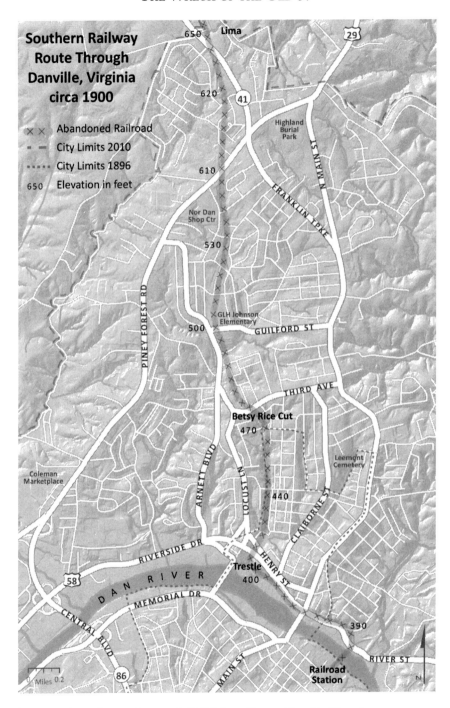

This map shows the actual route of Old 97 from Lima to Danville, Virginia, superimposed on a 2010 map of the city. *Courtesy of Melissa Dabbs and Corey Furches, GIS Division, Department of Information Technology, City of Danville, Virginia.*

was, having run freight trains across the trestle multiple times, both day and night. As he left Lima and followed the tracks to Stillhouse Trestle, there were several noteworthy descending grades.

Abundant trial testimony revealed what Broady knew about the last leg of the journey into Danville. Civil engineer and surveyor T.M. Bass testified that the steepest grade—about 2.0 percent—was next to Lima and extended a quarter of a mile. Farther down the track at the Betsy Rice Cut at Third Avenue, the grade was 1.5 percent. Both would have been pretty significant grades for a train. Bass explained, "Every 100 feet, with a one and a half percent grade, the road rises 18 inches higher at the end of the 100 feet than it was when you started." Bass could have added that it descends by the same amount going down.

If a train were going sixty miles per hour on a 1.5 percent grade, it would be going a mile a minute, or about 88 feet a second. About every second it would go down about sixteen inches on a descending grade. On a 2.0 percent grade, it would go down 1.8 feet every second and, in one minute, descend over 100 feet. Imagine an eighty-ton locomotive, a monstrous mass of iron, moving sixty miles per hour, pulling a fifty-three-ton tender and four cars, each weighing at least a minimum of fifty tons apiece. How far and how long would it take to stop such a train?

By the time the Old 97 got to Henry Street right above the trestle, the grade was about 1.0 percent on a curve going downhill. Taken together, the grades from Lima to the trestle averaged 1.5 percent with twists and turns along the way. This would not have been unfamiliar terrain, and "Steve" Broady would have been very aware that the trestle was coming up. If the air in his braking system was depleted, he would have been in charge of a runaway train.

C.S. Lake, trainmaster of the Danville Division, whose testimony has been cited earlier, stated that when Broady was hired, he cautioned him regarding "Danville as a location which should be approached cautiously, and it was very important that an engineer should understand that fact. I satisfied myself conclusively that he understood that fact."

W.W. Briggs, Southern's road foreman of engines, who had ridden some with Broady as he learned the road, testified that he had talked with Broady about his knowledge of the road, of the "physical conditions, and the approaching and handling of the engine from different points," and he specifically referred to coming into Danville. His advice to Broady: "Always approach it under control."

T.P. Bishop, Broady's engineer friend who came to Southern from Norfolk and Western at the same time as Broady, testified to the question: "What did he [Broady] say about Stillhouse Trestle?" Bishop replied, "He told me, when we were talking about approaches and things, to always come into Danville under control, and he did not like the stiff curve, and he said you did not want to approach that place too fast."

Thomas Bernard was Southern's road master in charge of the maintenance of the track for that section in 1903. He conceded at the trial that Southern Railway considered the wreck site "a bad entrance, and a bad grade, and a bad trestle." He also pointed out that because the railroad knew it was a bad place, it had put up a slow board nearby to prompt engineers to slow down at that point. In fact, it was probably the most dangerous spot in the entire Danville Division, even though no wrecks had occurred on the trestle before September 27, 1903.

By looking at his railroad watch—a type of watch renowned for its accuracy, requiring inspection regularly—Broady must have known at Lima that trying to make up any time before he reached Danville was useless. Why would he have made the decision at that point, with slightly over three miles to Danville and knowing the grades and curves, to push the train at such an abominable speed? Whatever the reason, Old 97 was speeding down the grade from Lima, definitely going faster than normal. And not only had Broady hardly made up any time, but time was also running out.

As Broady headed toward the trestle, his brother, George Broady, was still patiently waiting at the Danville Station, ready to deliver a letter from their mother. Steve Broady's brother would have known the train was late but was still unaware of impending danger.

Other folks were wondering what had happened to Old 97. Clay Keesee Pritchett remembered, "The train brought my Sunday paper, and it was late, so I went in the back room and stood up in a chair to see it make the famous curve for then I'd know how long it would be before I got my paper."

Jesse Giles, in an interview with the *Richmond Times-Dispatch* of June 6, 1953, stated that he was born on a farm but decided to quit "stirrin' the dirt" and went to Danville to work in the cloth room of the textile mill that was right next to the trestle. He was almost twenty-four years old on the day of the wreck. That Sunday was Giles's day off, and he had just visited his uncle Ches on "Arnett's hill," which he stated was about a quarter mile to one side of the trestle. Giles said, "While we [he and his Uncle Ches] were walking along Henry Street on the way to where I lived on Keen Street, [Old 97] just came along. It was behind schedule, you know."

John Lindsey Moore was still relaxing at the boardinghouse on the east side of Worsham Street in North Danville. Tipton Kodejs vividly recalled his grandfather's story about the famous train:

That Three-Mile Grade

After Sunday dinner men usually moved out on the front porch. There was no bridge then so you could see trains moving along the tracks. As Old 97 passed, the men would take out pocket watches and adjust their settings. On the afternoon of the wreck, the Old 97 was running late, and when they finally heard the train, my grandfather said, "You could tell by the sound that it was hauling the mail."

Earl Nostrandt, Robert Harris and Ned Williams were still playing marbles on Myrtle Avenue under the small maple tree when their attention turned to the train whistle. They had never heard it blow so long. Lawrence McFall wrote of his grandfather's experience:

The high banks where the train track came through the Betsy Rice Cut at Third Avenue made the whistle echo with an eerie scream. As the locomotive came nearer, the whistle continued its mournful sound. The lads jumped to their feet. They stood in awed silence. As the train passed within a few blocks, the youngsters knew that the menacing scream of that whistle surely meant something.

E.H. Chappell heard that sound, too. He had just awoken from his nap and was hot and thirsty, so he went outside to the well for water. In an article in *Retired Officer* magazine in May 1963, Chappell was quoted:

It was a roaring sound and while I couldn't see the track from where I stood because it ran through a deep fill at that point, I saw a great pillar of billowing dust, moving very fast. It was the train, of course, and she was making a weird, unusual noise. I remember I turned to my mother, who was with me, and said, "She'll never make the trestle."

In an interview for the *Danville Bee* dated September 26, 1953, Chappell said that the cloud of dust "looked a whirlwind moving fast." Chappell then dropped his bucket and ran.

Herman Lester and his cousin James had reached the crossing of the Southern mainline on Henry Street. James Lester later wrote:

I heard Old 97 coming down into Betsy Rice Cut about one-half mile from the crossing. I stopped to watch it pass as I had done many times. I saw that it was running much faster than usual at this point. I watched to see when the engineer would apply his brakes, and not until he had almost reached the crossing did I see sparks begin to fly from the brake shoes on the wheels. He was then some 75 yards from the sharp curve and trestle across the Old Stillhouse Branch. I knew he would never make the curve for he was making some 40–50 miles per hour.

According to Herman Lester's daughter, her father remembered his cousin saying, "Something's wrong. That train doesn't sound right."

Jordan recorded:

On Sunday afternoon, September 27, I went to the toilet, which was in the back of the garden near the railroad. When I came out, I heard a train coming. Knowing it was 97, I stopped to watch it. It was coming down the track running about 40 miles an hour, I imagined. Its whistle blew at what I thought was the Henry Street crossing. It passed me on its way to the trestle that made a curve to the left (going south).

A *Commercial Appeal* article of October 7, 1974, said that Amos Cass remembered walking south down the railroad that day and was on the verge of crossing the trestle when he heard the whistle break into a scream. He started to hurry down the embankment beside the trestle, but common sense told him he better not. He remembered that as the engine roared by, Broady appeared to have one hand on the air brake and one on the reverse bar.

A coroner's jury was held on September 28, the day after the wreck. Coroner William A. Baugh presided at the inquest held in the office of Constable F.M. Hamlin. John H. Falden of 906 Washington Street in Danville, a butcher, estimated that Old 97 was going thirty-five to forty miles per hour when it passed where he was standing, about three to four hundred yards from the trestle.

Commonwealth attorney Thomas Hamlin asked Falden, "Can you tell whether or not there were any brakes on the car or not?" Falden answered, "I do not think they were…I do not think the man had control of the train."

Another witness, W.Z. Morgan, a weaver, testified at the inquest that he thought the train was running fifty to sixty miles per hour but could not tell if the train was braking or not.

Also at the coroner's inquest, W.H. Mann of 38 John Street, said that he was twenty yards from the track as the train passed him. Hamlin asked Mann:

Q. What was the speed of the train at the time you saw it?
A. Sixty miles an hour, I suppose.

Q. Why do you think the train was running at a rate of 60 miles an hour?
A. I have a good deal of experience and can tell when trains are running fast.
Q. Did you see any of the men in charge of the train as it passed you?
A. Yes, sir. The engineer in his seat.
Q. Do you know whether or not the brakes were on and whether an attempt was made to slow up the train?
A. They did not seem to be making any attempt. He was perfectly quiet in his seat.
Q. Did you hear any bell ring or whistle blow?
A. He blew station above the crossing, can't say how far away.

John C. Wiley and Ethel Faust were still enjoying the beautiful day, sitting on the grassy banks of Reservoir Hill about fifty yards above the track, when they heard the train. Wiley stated that the train's whistle was barely audible above the rumble. "We weren't particularly waitin' for the train, but we knowed it was past due coming in." At age ninety-three, Wiley clearly remembered, "I knowed when I heard that whistle it was goin' too fast." Wiley estimated the speed at seventy-five miles an hour.

Daisy Willis, who was eating Sunday dinner with her family that day, heard the train coming and felt the ground shake from the vibration of the speeding train. She said, "Daddy, I don't think the train will ever make the crossing." Her father replied, "Aw shucks, you don't know what you're talking about. Eat your dinner."

There were other children who were about to witness the wreck. Dewey Davis had been pulling his younger brother, Claude, in a small wagon near the wreck site and had stopped to watch the train go by. Lewis Owen and a friend were playing under the trestle and looked up when they heard the train approaching. Other accounts say the children were those of Rufus Jones.

Despite the differences in estimates of the train's speed, almost everyone who heard the train remembers that screaming whistle. Mr. E.F. Carter, who lived nearby, also described a long whistle blast: "It was the most horrible sound I ever heard."

Pat Fox sums up the awful moments before the wreck:

The whistle…gave a series of blasts on the approach to Lima and finally set up a constant broken wailing down the three-mile grade to the Dan Valley. It was the death cry of a runaway locomotive and it chilled the hearts of all who heard it. People turned in their yards, ran out on their porches, stopped still along the streets in North Danville. All eyes turned in the direction of the approaching train. With bated breath and anxious hearts, they waited.

The engineer would normally have blown the whistle at a crossing such as Henry Street, but that day it appeared to sound different. People gathered that something was wrong and something bad was about to happen. Would Old 97 make the trestle? That was the question on everyone's mind. And it was about to be answered.

STILLHOUSE TRESTLE

It [Old 97] *just split the curve.*
—John Wiley, eyewitness

As Old 97 rolled across the crossing at Henry Street, Stillhouse Trestle loomed in front of locomotive 1102 like the gaping mouth of a hungry dragon. Local folks who lived with the trains passing over the trestle day and night were used to the speed and sound of the train and knew when something was wrong. That was especially true on that Sunday, when Old 97 was so late. Hardly anyone who saw or heard the train on its final approach to the trestle believed it could avoid wrecking.

Stillhouse Trestle got its name from the creek that bears the name. One story says that a mayor of Danville, James M. Walker, owned a store on Danville's Main Street and a distillery on the north side of the Dan River at the trestle. Another story says that the creek was named after Cobb's Still House, which had an operation at the spring source of the creek. And yet another story claims that the still house for which the trestle was named was that of the K.C. Arey Company. Regardless, a distillery there belonged to someone, so it naturally came to be called Stillhouse Creek.

The creek or branch, obviously a necessary source of water for the distillery, was not large. Over many eons, it had cut a steep ravine through the hard bedrock, some of which was a billion or more years old. As it wound its way down the hillside and under the trestle, it flowed onward into the Dan

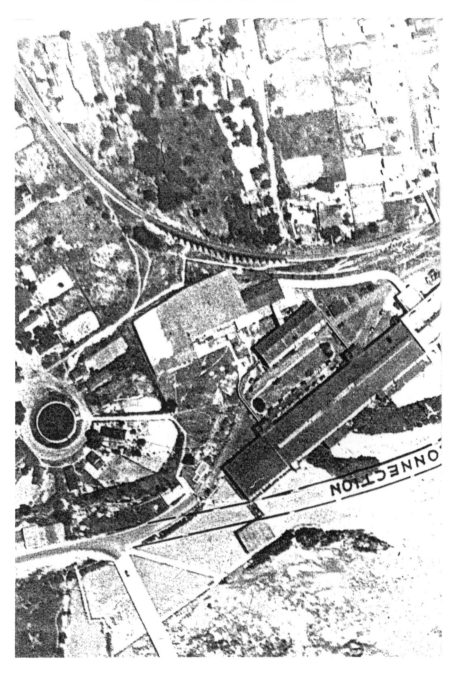

Aerial view of the Old 97 wreck site, with Stillhouse Trestle slightly above the center of photo.

River. Stillhouse Creek, or Stillhouse Branch as it is sometimes referred to, can still be seen today, as can part of the ravine.

The trestle, at 282 feet, spanned the ravine as the track proceeded from the Henry Street crossing, with the curvature of the track beginning about two to three hundred feet north of the trestle. Elevated on the right, or western, side about three and a half inches, the trestle curved down and to the left. After leaving the trestle, the track leveled out and followed the river, then rounded a curve and crossed the river over a bridge into Danville Station.

At its highest point above the ravine, the wooden trestle rose forty-five feet. It was made of units called bents, each composed of upright and angled beams, with each unit joined together in succession by horizontal and crisscrossing timbers.

Stillhouse Trestle had been there since 1874, and the trestle had never collapsed from trains running across it. Further, no accident like that of September 27, 1903, had ever occurred previously. Even so, three months before the wreck, a civil engineer working for Southern Railway, James I. Lee of Lynchburg, drew up plans on June 17, 1903, for filling up the ravine

Stillhouse Trestle looking toward the north. The arrow in the background points to the railroad crossing sign at Henry Street. *Photo courtesy of Clara Fountain.*

under the trestle. Had this task been completed that summer, it would have changed the scenery at the trestle and perhaps the outcome of the wreck.

Frame houses, easily visible from the trestle, dotted the hillsides and nearby streets. Cotton mill buildings were located on the western side of the trestle and along the tracks that paralleled the Dan River. A culvert had been constructed in the bank beyond the trestle to allow the shallow creek to flow under the mill storage building. It was there that Southern's Fast Mail train ended its journey.

As Old 97 neared the trestle, a warning sign notified engineers to slow down. According to trial testimony, a slow board was located forty-five feet north of milepost 237, or about sixteen hundred feet from the trestle. This three- by four-foot sign with letters six and one-quarter inches high featured the word "SLOW." Engineers were required to obey the speed rule, in this case Rule No. 7 from page 183 of the rule book that Broady had studied for his examination: "Speed of passenger trains will not exceed forty five miles per hour over truss bridges or viaducts…Speed of passenger trains will not exceed fifteen miles per hour over structures protected by slow boards."

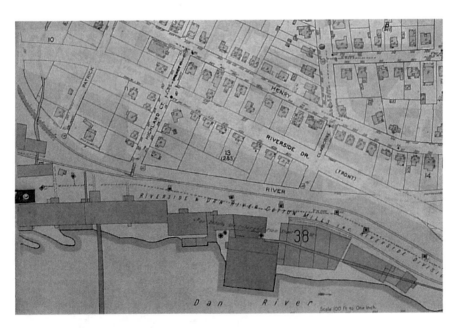

This map section shows the trestle area with mill buildings along the river at the bottom. Stillhouse Trestle is located on the far left slightly above center. *From a book titled* Insurance Maps of Danville, Virginia, *published by the Sanborn Map Company of New York. Courtesy of Lawrence McFall.*

Since Old 97 was classified as a passenger train, it was required to slow down to fifteen miles per hour over the trestle. However, 1905 trial testimony noted that at twenty to twenty-five miles per hour the train should still be able to cross safely.

Before approaching the trestle, it was also required that engineers be sure that they could adequately slow down to the necessary speed. Superintendent Coapman read into court records Rule No. 544:

> *In approaching fixed signals, railroad crossings at grade, draw bridges, meeting points, yard limits which they are required by rule to regard, caution signs, heavy descending grades, and other dangerous or doubtful places, when far enough therefrom to admit of stopping or slowing the train, as the circumstances may require, by manual application of the brakes, they must test the air brakes, and if they do not work effectively, they must call for their application by hand in time to insure the stopping of the train before passing the danger point, or its proper control before passing the caution point.*

Whether Broady did this or not remains an unanswered question, but it appears from the following testimony that he did not.

F.G. Brooks, a postal clerk in the last car, had been sorting the mail ever since leaving Lynchburg, "going through the stalls and getting it in shape for dispatch." He testified in the 1905 trial that at the trestle Old 97 "was running faster than I have ever known it to run before. I have oftentimes taken notice of trains and got some idea of running and I think it was running a mile a minute."

Brooks added, "It slows up always; I have never known it to go across there so fast," meaning across the trestle. "We can tell when they [trains] slow up; we can feel the brakes. Anyone standing can feel it more perceptively than one sitting down." Brooks told the court that he did not believe that Old 97 "checked up"—that is, slowed—since Lynchburg.

N.C. Maupin, a postal clerk in the second car behind the engine or the first mail car behind the express car, testified, "It always slowed up before going on the trestle. I remember that; we always felt the air. I didn't feel the air come down on it and didn't feel it check up." In an interview, Steve Maupin, the grandson of N.C. Maupin, told me, "I remember him telling me he knew the engineer was going too fast for the trestle and thought about jumping from the train, but realized the train was going too fast."

Charles E. Reames, also in the first mail car, testified in court that he thought Old 97 "was going 60 mile an hour or more. I have ridden trains a good many times since I have been in the service, and I have timed trains occasionally, and got some idea of how fast trains are running." Reames was asked, "Had he checked up at all as he came down to Danville?" He responded, "No, sir, I didn't notice any check since he left Lynchburg. The first check I noticed was when we went over the trestle."

A.R. Creasy, the section foreman for the line between Lima and the north end of the Danville Branch, had been working for Southern ever since its inception. His house was about one-half mile or about twenty-five hundred feet north of the trestle. In the court proceedings, Creasy was asked:

> Q. Did you see the train when it passed your house?
> A. Yes, sir.
> Q. How fast was the train running?
> A. I don't know; it was running very fast.
> Q. Did you notice its speed?
> A. I think it was running a little faster than usual.

Under cross-examination, Creasy was questioned further:

> Q. Don't all those fast trains on the Southern Rwy pass by your house at a lively rate of speed?
> A. Yes, sir, but not as fast as that.
> Q. You think this was a little livelier than the general run of them?
> A. Yes, sir, I know it.

The testimonies above suggest that when Old 97 reached the slow board and continued toward the trestle, it neither slowed up nor exercised any braking power. They also support the idea that the train was running at least sixty miles per hour.

D.W. Lumm, a civil engineer who had worked for Southern for twenty years and was its chief engineer of maintenance of way and structures, added the following remark in court testimony:

> The speed of 60 miles per hour on a ten-degree curve would cause the engine to topple over in its course forward, and would raise the inner wheels above the stop rail or mainline rail…at 60 miles per hour the inner wheels would not be on the rails at all.

Lumm noted further that there were markings on the outer end of the ties on the western side of the trestle, "a short distance from the end of the trestle," and no marks between the ties.

Lumm's observations and those of others show that engine 1102 left the track fifty-one feet before the trestle and ran along the crossties with the left drivers lifted off the track (with possibly the front truck wheels still on) while the right drivers bumped along the crossties. When the locomotive got to the trestle, the right drivers continued bumping along on the trestle ties until the locomotive lunged off with the left drivers striking the trestle rails and timbers, rolling the engine toward its left side. The track was torn up about thirty-five to forty feet into the trestle as the train decoupled and launched off the four-story rise.

For a brief moment, in less time than it takes to read this sentence, Old 97, with its four cars and its crew, hung suspended in space above the creek bed. Then it crashed.

THE FATAL PLUNGE

I never seen anything skeetin' through the air like he was.
—Jesse Giles, eyewitness

It was a perfect fall afternoon when Old 97, like an arrow shot from a bow, plunged into the ravine below Stillhouse Trestle. James I. Robertson, in an August 1958 article in the *Virginia Cavalcade*, described the wreck as follows:

> With a thud and roar never before heard in Danville, the engine's left side struck the creek bed; she half-buried herself in the mud, the drive wheels continuing to turn slowly. As steam spewed from every direction, the four cars tumbled and shattered almost on top of the overturned locomotive.

It was a spectacular ending to a short history that had begun barely a year before. But for the people who saw it, it would be long on memory.

With the mail ready to be unloaded at Danville, Jennings J. Dunlap was resting on some sacks at the rear of his postal car. As the train launched over the trestle, Dunlap believed that being in the back of the car on those sacks "probably saved me. There were five in our car. Two were killed and two others hurt." Dunlop later claimed in a newspaper interview about the wreck, "It happened too fast to get scared. In a split second the train was falling apart and there were splinters everywhere."

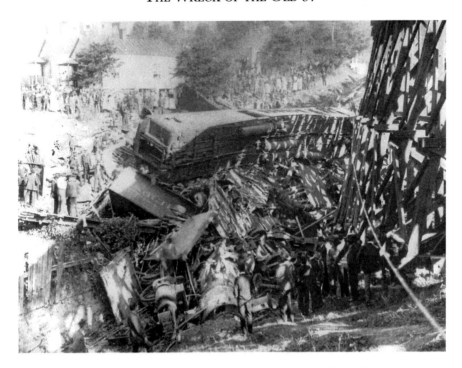

A view of the wreck site on the Monday morning after the wreck. Notice that the second driving wheel on the exposed side of the engine is missing a metal ring, called a tire—a likely cause of the derailment. *Photo courtesy of Howard Gregory.*

Postal clerk J. Harris Thompson said:

> *I could feel the cars rocking and swaying. In the end coach, we naturally caught most of the motion, and I'm not ashamed to admit that I and everyone else in the car was plenty scared.*
>
> *I was standing at the back door of the rear car, holding on to the [mail] catcher arm. The train rolled onto the curved, five-decker trestle and left the track at 2:43 p.m. I can hear that glass from the windows shattering over me yet as the train plunged into the ravine.*

Postal clerk N.C. Maupin was asked in the 1905 trial about the moment of the wreck:

> *Q. What were you doing?*
> *A. When they went over I was standing up between the double doors, just coming into Danville. I wasn't doing anything.*

Q. What did you find next?
A. The next, I heard a crash and I remember the car just dropped over the trestle.
Q. Which way did she turn?
A. It turned over on this side.
Q. Towards the west.
A. Towards the cotton mills.
Q. That was the first you knew?
A. I just heard a crash and the car toppled over.

Omie Gibbs, a little girl picking flowers near the trestle at the moment of the wreck, remembered in later years:

> *The whole train began to bend and buckle like a snake and it moaned just before it reached the trestle…When the train hit the trestle, the cars left the track, and they took the engine with them into the streambed.*

Joe Morgan, a night watchman who lived close by, recalled:

> *When Old 97 came down toward the trestle, I was looking right at it. It flew right off. Telephone poles flew higher than the trestle. I can see that train going off now. That engine jumped before it got to the trestle and it jumped somewhere around 300 feet. It jumped from the end of the trestle to the middle of the bank. I can see it clear now. I will never forget that day.*

John Wiley, standing on the knoll with Ethel Faust, was quoted in a *Danville Register* article on September 25, 1988:

> *The engine went first, splintering a telegraph pole and sailing about 100 feet before thudding into the mud. Each of the cars behind came crashing on top of the engine—one, two, three, four—pounding it into the earth. The last, cushioned by the debris of those before, was the only car not destroyed. Right then, there was a loud sound, an explosion just like a firecracker, which was a busted boiler or something. Steam was everywhere.*

In another interview for the *Danville Bee* in September 1976, Wiley noted:

> *[Old 97] blowed for the Henry Street crossing and was going so fast you didn't have time to wink your eyes before it hit the trestle—just split the*

The wreck scene with the corner of the mill building (top left), engine 1102 on its side (bottom right) and, to its left, part of the wall of the culvert that channeled water from the creek under the mill building.

curve. A telephone pole at the curve beside the trestle was splintered like a toothpick as the cars and engine plunged off the trestle into the creek bed and struck an abutment of a culvert that carried the creek water under the Dan River storage building.

Wiley described the scene again in the *Danville Weekender* on the anniversary of the wreck, September 27, 1980:

The engineer was running so fast he couldn't make the curve. It all happened so dad-blamed quick I couldn't tell if he was trying to slow down or not. But he was really goin' up there in speed. When he came around the curve, he jumped the track and sailed into the ravine below. I figure he was running about 85–90 miles an hour. When he sailed off the track his speed was checked by a light pole he ran into. If he hadn't hit it he would have gone right into the [mill storage] *building.*

The Fatal Plunge

A previously unpublished photo of the wreck of Old 97 showing the engine still on its side with the remains of mail cars behind it. *Courtesy Greensboro Chapter National Railway Historical Society.*

Herman Lester and his cousin James were also eyewitnesses. Herman recalled, "It looked like a bomb had hit a building. Smoke and steam were everywhere. The impact of the wreck was so strong that the engine was buried in the mud." His cousin James remembered, "The cars were lapped over like dominoes and crushed in like orange crates."

Also at the wreck were Jessie Wilmer Giles and his uncle Ches. They had been seconds away from being hit by 97 as it came down toward the trestle. Giles said that they "jumped the track" just before Old 97 sped by. Giles, at age seventy-four in an interview with the *Richmond Times-Dispatch*, said, "If we'd been two seconds later that afternoon, we'd have been killed, too." He continued:

> *We crossed the tracks when it came along…*[Old 97] *came by us ps-s-s-shew, just coming like a bullet. That thing was coming so fast, brother,*

it wasn't makin' any noise—just like a puff of wind. The only fuss it made was just before it got to the trestle. It sounded like he'd just reversed his engine. It was out of control, no doubt about that...He could have been going 90 all right...I never seen anything skeetin' through the air like he was...It looked like the cars just dumped into the ravine one right on top of another.

With the locomotive in the creek and the cars piled in a heap of rubble, Giles and his uncle Ches headed down to help:

We scrambled down the bluff and tried to get the crippled out. I don't remember how many we brought out—several. One man, a mail clerk, who lived in Spencer, wanted to send a telegram to his wife. He dictated it to me. Brave? His head was the soundest part of him—his legs were broken, his arms; he was hurt in the chest. When he finished he went unconscious and died.

They worked until 9:00 p.m. that night, also helping pick up the mail. Giles reiterated that he had always been a timid man, but that Sunday afternoon made a distinct impression that lasted his whole life. "As long as I lived I hoped I'd never see anything else like it."

Accompanied by his brothers on the hill a short distance from the trestle, six-year-old Ruel Bullington saw the wreck, recalling his experience for the *Danville Bee* on September 27, 1963. The roar of the engine grew louder and suddenly came into view on the boys' right, with the earth shaking beneath them. Bullington said:

Out onto the trestle the engine started ripping rails. There was a terrible noise and it couldn't make it around. The engine and then the cars went off the far side. You could have heard the noise all the way to Schoolfield Mills. Then it was silent. The whole ravine was filled with dust. At first we couldn't see anything. Then we could make out that awful mess. I was scared...trembling. I've never been as scared in my life.

E.H. Chappell, who dropped his water bucket and ran toward the trestle when he heard the train's awful sound coming down the track, remembered the loud metallic noises; saw rising steam, dust and flames; and heard the cries of those who were hurt when he got to the scene. Howard Gregory wrote in his history of the wreck:

The Fatal Plunge

When [Chappell] *arrived on the scene, the dust was still thick in the air with steam escaping from a torn cylinder on one side of the locomotive. Some of the injured were crawling out of the wreckage while others were sitting on the ground with their heads in their hands. Dr. L.L. Vann* [was] *walking among the injured, administering hypodermics.*

Chappell said that some of the injured were laid on a grassy bank on mattresses provided by nearby residents; they twisted in pain with their clothing in rags. An injured man on one of the mattresses asked John Wiley for a pencil and paper, and after writing a short note to his wife, he laid his head back and died.

Mark Daniel Jones was awakened from his Sunday afternoon nap by the long, continuous steam whistle of the train coming down the distant hill. He told his pregnant wife, Annie, that something was wrong. According to his grandson, Danny Rickets:

He stepped out of a low window and starting running towards the tracks which were about four blocks away. After running down John Street (now Richmond Avenue) one block, he was crossing Claiborne Street when he saw a cloud of dust rise and heard the rumbling crash. The noise lasted a while when the cars crushed on top of one another.

Rickets said his grandfather remembered the mill bells and church bells ringing. "Everybody knew something really terrible had happened." Jones was the third man to reach the wreck and helped with rescue efforts.

Dr. C.J. Carter saw the wreck from his front porch. He sent a message to the stationmaster in Danville telling him that Old 97 had wrecked at the trestle. Though he hesitated to believe it, the stationmaster heard the bells, saw the crowds headed in that direction and ran toward the trestle himself.

The watchman at the mill sounded a fire alarm. S.I. Roberts, superintendent of Riverside Mills, got to the wreck in a few minutes. He said:

I have an alarm in the house and my orders is if there is a fire near the mill to ring the bell. They rung the bell in probably two minutes, and I went up there as fast as I could go. It was Sunday and I had my slippers on; I didn't stop to take them off.

The mill bell and church bells ringing, later joined by the bell at the courthouse in Danville, made a melancholy choir chiming a funeral dirge amid the fury of fire and smoke. Fortunately, the fire was short lived. It is said that the mill fire department arrived on the scene, as did the Danville Fire Department with its fire wagon pulled by horses. Even though the firemen were able to extinguish the fire that the engine's firebox had ignited in the wreckage, steam still continued to come out of the punctured engine.

People poured from their houses "like a swarm of bees." Some say that thousands surrounded the site. When the congregation in the church Oscar Hardy was attending on Keen Street heard the horrible sound, no one paid much attention to the sermon. Afterward, all of the church members ran down the hill toward the wreck as fast as they could. At Will Payne's church, the scorching sermon on sin and destruction was cut short by the loud earth-shaking explosions of the train's crash. The sound brought the congregation members out of their seats and turned them into "a rioting mob."

David Luther, Danville city councilman, related that his grandfather, Gaines P. Luther, moved to Danville in 1903, and the family lived on Dame

Posing atop the wreckage of Old 97 is a Danville police officer (back left with badge), section foreman William B. Gosney (kneeling in foreground) and, behind him, Mark Daniel Jones, the third person to arrive at the wreck scene. *Photo courtesy of Clara Fountain.*

Bystanders after the wreck gaze at the locomotive half buried and covered with debris. The Railway Post Office car lies on top of the wreckage. The last car on the train, it sustained less damage than the others and was eventually repaired. *Photo courtesy of Clara Fountain.*

Street. His grandfather worked as a weaver at the mill but wasn't working the day of the wreck. Luther recalled his grandfather saying that he heard the mill bell start ringing and that people were everywhere.

The Danville Police Department responded within a few minutes to find the wreck scene a horrifying experience for many. Some ladies who drove out in buggies supposedly fainted at the sight of badly mangled bodies. It was reported later that a woman had a miscarriage. A Richmond newspaper noted that "a woman in a delicate condition of health witnessed the wreck from her chamber window. She fell to the floor unconscious and it is not believed she will live." Regardless of how factual the stories and how traumatic the events, the wreck scene was aptly described in another newspaper article as "weird beyond description."

With downed telegraph lines hindering communication with railroad stations north of the wreck, W.H. Mann, an employee in the boiler room of the cotton mill, grabbed a red flag and hurried up the track to flag down a freight train that was supposedly following Old 97. Other southbound trains had to be rerouted around the unusable trestle. Until it was repaired,

Another image of the wreck scene photographed by Leon Taylor of Danville. *Photo courtesy of Howard Gregory, who reprinted it with permission of Williams Studios of Danville.*

Southern trains were diverted from Lynchburg on Norfolk and Western Railway lines through Appomattox, Virginia, to Burkeville. From there, they were run to Danville over Southern's Richmond–Danville line.

Cars were splintered into kindling wood—except the last car, which landed on the others. Haunting cries came from the carnage. Circling around the engine, flying back and forth and chirping loudly, were canaries, whose express car crates had been cracked open by the impact.

John Lindsey Moore, who had been sitting on the front porch of the boardinghouse on Worsham Street when Old 97 jumped the trestle, said, "It was the most awful sound I've heard in my life. The sound shook the house. It seemed to go on and on." Despite being dressed in a gentleman's three-piece suit, Moore took off to the wreck site. "I nearly ran myself to death that day." When he got there, he remarked, "It was one big mess. These yellow canaries were everywhere."

Earl Nostrandt and his friends ran toward the mountainous cloud of dust and the hissing noise of steam escaping the engine. One of the canaries flittering about wildly almost landed on Earl's shoulder. Earl stayed at the site until darkness fell and the lanterns were brought out. Joe Morgan also remembered the canaries flying all around. His mother, like other folks, caught one and kept it as a pet. Gaines P. Luther remembered that some people put them in cages.

Supposedly, the canaries were headed to West Virginia coal mines, where they were to be used to warn miners of odorless poisonous gases in their workspace. If the deadly gases overcame the canaries, they would stop chirping. That would serve as a silent warning for the miners to leave. It is ironic that the wreck that caused the deaths of so many and the destruction of a train may in fact have saved the lives of those canaries.

Jesse Giles, who, along with his uncle, had barely escaped being hit, recalled, "I never saw as many canaries and parrots in my life. Their cages were smashed and they were everywhere. And these actor's suits—big beaver hats and split-tail coats."

Also in the express car was a wooden crate of special-order cut flowers from Philadelphia destined for H.W. Brown Florist in Danville. Despite the catastrophic destruction that afternoon, the contents had remained intact. Dud Brown, son of H.W. Brown, found the crate, making it possible to deliver the Monday morning orders on schedule. The florist is still a prominent business in Danville.

L.C. Jordan, who had been walking in his backyard, leapt the fence, reached the wreck and saw a young man on his back, pinned beneath the side of a mail car. It was Scott Chambers, who had been recently married. Chambers had tried to free himself with his one free elbow, but Jordan finally freed him and dragged him up onto the bank. Chambers told Jordan to write down his name and address. While Jordan took a pencil out of his pocket and went to get a wooden plank from the wreck, Chambers died.

Jordan rushed to help another man trying to pry one of the injured loose—the clerk Daniel P. Flory. The men removed the steel and boards from over Flory and then lifted him to the creek bank, but he remained silent. He, too, was dead.

Daisy Willis and her father stopped eating Sunday dinner when the dishes on the table started vibrating from the impact of the wreck. They ran to the to the wreck site and helped with the rescue. As they dug through the wreckage, they uncovered another mail clerk, P.M. Argenbright. Daisy's father ran to the creek to scoop up water while Daisy held the bleeding man's head in her lap. Returning from the creek with a rusty can filled with water, her father greeted a corpse. Argenbright also died.

John Thompson, the mail clerk in charge, was found in the last car, a metal shaft protruding through his shoulder blades. He was shouting insanely and did not want to leave since the mail was his responsibility. He was, nevertheless, taken from the wreckage, but he died on the way to the Home for the Sick on Jefferson Street.

J. Harris Thompson, no relation to John Thompson, was interviewed by M.W. Paxton in Lexington, Virginia, for a newspaper article on the fiftieth anniversary of the wreck. Thompson had been standing next to the mail catcher arm on the last car and recalled that horrifying moment:

> *I crawled out on top of the car and Dunlap pulled me away from the wreck. I could see fire starting up in the wreckage. I lay on a mattress on the hill from a little after 2 p.m. until 5 p.m. before they tried to move me…A thing like that leaves you with a mental picture you never lose.*

His clothes were torn to shreds, his hip was dislocated and blood poured down his side from lacerations. Thompson regained consciousness at about 5:00 p.m., lying on a mattress in the shade of a nearby front porch.

Barney Lawless, whose mail clerk grandfather, Clarence Goodloe, had aimed to catch Old 97 before it left Washington, remembered meeting J. Harris Thompson in 1952, when he (Lawless) was a cadet at Virginia Military Institute in Lexington, Virginia. It seems that Lawless and several other cadets were headed down to Woody's Chevrolet body shop, where every Saturday night those who wanted to could sing for silver dollars.

Lawless and his friends had gone over to his girlfriend's house on Jackson Avenue to practice their theme song: "The Wreck of the Old 97." His girlfriend's father told him that right across the street lived a survivor of that wreck, J. Harris Thompson. Lawless, about eighteen or nineteen years old at the time, got to talk to Thompson face to face about the famous incident. Thompson told Lawless that he had known his grandfather, who regularly rode on Old 97 and sometimes helped train postal clerks on that run.

Concerning the wreck, Thompson told Lawless that Old 97 got to the top of the hill and ignored a slow board sign. Thompson said that he and three others had jumped off the train. He ended up with a broken collarbone and shoulder blade. According to Thompson, he lay there all night and wasn't found until sometime the next day.

The two conflicting stories conveyed by J. Harris Thompson are difficult to reconcile, especially since it is questionable that anyone jumped. However, we must accept them at face value—the conflicts perhaps due to a hazy memory.

The Fatal Plunge

W.F. Pinckney, the express messenger, was sitting on the safe in the car behind the engine when the impact occurred. John Wiley saw both the mail train safe and Pinckney hurled out the car door. The impact stunned Pinckney, and the safe's door was thrown open, with thousands of dollars worth of bills spilling all over the ground. John Wiley said that Pinckney ran around "like he was out of his senses" and then stopped to pick up the money and return it to the safe.

According to another source, Pinckney was asked by a bystander if this was his first wreck. He retorted that it was his second and last. He stayed with the money until a horse and wagon took him and the safe to a Danville hotel for the night (it was Sunday and no banks were open). The next day, he rode a train to Charlotte and mailed in his resignation.

An article in the *Richmond News Leader* the day after the wreck reported that Pinckney saw the safe locker Wentworth Armistead across the car from him as the train toppled over the trestle. Armistead, being in the express car, the first one behind the engine, was found buried beneath the sprawling wreckage.

Along with contents of the safe, the mail from postal cars was scattered about the wreck, although most was intact. R.B. Boulding, a mail clerk, arrived a short time later and took charge of the mail. Mail clerks were also sent on special trains from Richmond, Charlottesville and Greensboro, North Carolina, and Atlanta, Georgia, to rescue the government property and re-sort the mail.

According to his grandson Steve Maupin, postal clerk N.C. Maupin was trapped by a bolt through the second finger of one of his hands. "He was buried in the wreckage and at one time asked for a knife from the rescuers so he could cut his finger off and get free." The rescuers promised to give him the knife if they couldn't get him out. However, the men were successful in removing Maupin with his finger intact.

In the same car as Maupin was clerk Charles E. Reames, who told the *Virginia Star* of Culpepper in an interview published August 10, 1933, "I was catapulted through the side [of the second postal car] and landed thirty feet away. The sun was shining on me when I opened my eyes." Though described as "battered, bruised and unconscious" at first, he survived.

Although some of the postal workers lived, the majority died immediately or shortly after the wreck. Postal clerk Lewis W. Spies, according to Pat Fox's history of the wreck, was found beside a pile of heavy iron; his head had been torn open by a steel slab. He was conscious and able to talk when he was removed from the wreck but remained in critical condition.

The most gruesome accounts of the disaster relate to the engine and train crew that boarded at Monroe. That group included Broady, Hodge, Clapp, Blair and Moody.

A September 26, 1976 *Commercial Appeal* article gives the account of Gracie Mae Whitman, then ninety-four and living in Jacksonville, Florida. When she was twenty-one, she and her family moved to Danville to work in the cotton mill and rented a house on Front Street. According to Whitman, on that Sunday afternoon, people were wearing their Sunday best waiting for the train's arrival—always the biggest event of the week.

When the wreck took place, she said, "I went running to the ravine to see what had happened. There was the twisted wreckage of the engine and the mail cars." Whitman saw many bodies mangled and scalded from the steam. She recalled recognizing the engineer because of his white shirt and another man, who was bleeding and told her not to bother with him but help someone else.

John Wiley saw engineer Broady tumbling out of one side of the engine while the two firemen were thrown out on the other side. It is likely that the firemen were killed on impact rather than scalded to death by steam alone. Howard Gregory wrote that "both firemen [Buddy Clapp and John Hodge] were thrown out of the left side of the engine, scalded and mangled beyond recognition, dying instantly."

Wiley recalled in a *Danville Bee* article in September 1976 that Broady collapsed in Stillhouse Creek. "I helped pick the engineer up," he said.

> *The skin* [and hair] *came off his arm just like a chicken that's scalded. Somebody came from the houses above, and two or three men helped me pick up the engineer and put him on the bank. He drawed two or three breaths and that was the end of him.*

Claims have been made that Broady cried out, "Cut my leg off! Get me out! I'm scalding to death." However, Wiley noted in a September 27, 1980 article for the *Danville Register and Bee Weekender* that "he didn't say nothing." Wiley further stated, "Somebody had claimed that he [Broady] had lost a leg. But I didn't see nothing like that."

Herman Lester was there when the engineer was pulled from the wreckage, and his memory adds more detail. In an interview for the November 6, 1994 Sunday edition of the *Danville Register and Bee*, Lester remembered, "His skin was black from the fire and steam. He couldn't talk. People were asking him his name. He pointed to his chest and pulled out his wallet. He died shortly after that." Broady's brother George arrived at the scene and maintained a vigil beside the lifeless body.

Conductor Blair was found underneath the mass of steel beams, wooden beams and mail bags. He was alive when he was pulled out but died on the way to the hospital.

Flagman J.T. Moody was reportedly found at the crest of the ridge, farther uphill than the others. James I. Robertson's account of the wreck states:

> *Sensing the impending disaster, Moody had leaped from the train just as it swerved off the track. He had fallen heavily to the ground dislocating a shoulder, but he remained conscious and had thus seen the train carry the others to their deaths.*

Robertson adds that Moody was in shock when others reached him. He grappled violently with several men and was half subdued with a heavy rope. Dr. Carter administered morphine to Moody, who died a few hours later.

At the home of eight-year-old Greenhow Maury, who had finished lunch and gone outside to play, the phone rang. Ninety-four-year-old Maury, in an interview with the *Richmond Times-Dispatch*, recalled the message, "It was my Uncle Rutherford Harvie saying 97 had jumped the trestle by the Long Mill. We hot-footed it down to the wreck, which was about two miles away."

Maury's grandfather, Dr. Lewis E. Harvie, had been called since he was the Southern Railway surgeon. By the time they got there, most of the bodies had been removed from the wreckage and covered with sheets. Maury stated that he remembered seeing the bodies of Broady and the firemen. "Every now and then a sheet would be pulled back so people could see."

News of the disaster also arrived by telephone on Cabell Street. After hearing that Old 97 wrecked, eleven-year-old Myrtle Poole, her older sister Viola and their parents boarded an already packed streetcar in front of their house. The family had gone to the Episcopal church that morning, and the girls still had on their Sunday dresses. After the streetcar crossed the Main Street Bridge, passengers debarked and walked up the south end of the trestle to the wreck. As Myrtle looked down, she saw white sheets along the hillside. Lawrence McFall added that his grandmother, "when told that they covered dead bodies, closed her eyes and refused to open them."

The sights and sounds on that Sunday afternoon destroyed not only the train but also whatever charm the day would have held. The crashing sound and shaking ground; the dust, debris, smoke and fire; the mournful cries of wounded and dying men; the sheet-covered bodies on mattresses; the wagons hauling the wounded to the Home for the Sick; the proud locomotive steeped in mud; and the postal cars shredded like paper—all created a surreal scene. For a host of onlookers, that serene Sunday afternoon became a nightmare to remember.

THE MOURNING AFTER

I knowed it was a bad wreck when I seen it.
—John Wiley, eyewitness

As night cast a veil of darkness over the gruesome scene created by the wreck of Old 97, flares and lanterns hung on trees and poles. The headlight of an engine backed onto the trestle lit up the crushed cars and helpless engine. The crowds dissipated, except for those few who continued searching for the dead and dying.

By late Sunday evening, all of the bodies, except that of Wentworth Armistead, were accounted for. Most of the dead had died immediately or soon after the wreck. All of the engine and train crew were dead: Joseph Andrew Broady, thirty-three, of Saltville, Virginia; conductor John Thomas Blair, thirty-seven, of Spencer, North Carolina; fireman A.C. "Buddy" Clapp, thirty-three, of Whitsett, North Carolina; apprentice fireman John Marshall Hodge, twenty-one, of Raleigh, North Carolina; and flagman J.S. Moody, thirty, of Raleigh, North Carolina.

Postal clerks who died that day were J.L. Thompson, thirty-six, of Washington, D.C.; Scott Chambers, twenty-four, of Midland, Virginia; Daniel P. Flory, twenty-five, of Nokesville, Virginia; Paul N. Argenbright, twenty-three, of Mount Clinton, Virginia; and Lewis W. Spies, thirty-four, of Manassas, Virginia, who died nearly a week later, on October 6.

The injured were Frank E. Brooks, forty-four, of Charlottesville, Virginia; Percival Indermauer, twenty-seven, of Washington, D.C.; Charles E.

Reames, thirty-eight, of Culpeper, Virginia; Jennings J. Dunlap, twenty-three, of Norwood, North Carolina; Napoleon C. Maupin, twenty-three, of Charlottesville, Virginia; and J. Harris Thompson, twenty-four, of St. Luke, Virginia. Express messenger W.R. Pinckney was listed as uninjured with a few scratches.

About 11:00 p.m. on Sunday night, work crews began repairing the wooden trestle and tracks on the damaged area where Old 97 had launched out into the ravine. Two and a half hours after the wreck, N.L. Hall, Southern's supervisor of bridges and buildings, arrived at the site and took charge of the repairs. Repairs took all night, and by 8:30 a.m. on Monday, the trestle had been repaired. The first train inched its way across less than an hour later.

The body of Wentworth Armistead, the youngster who was not able to get off the train in time at Lynchburg, was still in the wreckage on Monday morning. According to Raymond Carneal's account, Armistead's brothers, Henry Armistead of Salisbury and Louis Armistead of Lamberts Point, Virginia, were there to help search for his body. The seventeen-year-old Armistead had been in the express car directly behind the engine along with Pinckney. His car went off the trestle first, and the other cars crashed, splintered and piled on top of it.

Later Monday morning, Armistead was found at the bottom of the wreckage. Along with his brothers, who had arrived previously, Wentworth's father, Samuel, of the Lynchburg Fire Department; his mother; and his little brother, Albert, were also there when Wentworth's body was found.

Also on that Monday, W.W. Finley, vice-president for Southern Railway, issued the following statement:

> *This train consisted of two postal cars, one express car and one baggage car for the storage of mail. The trestle is very little damaged as the train jumped the track about 40 feet north of the trestle on sound track, good line and surface and proper gauge. The trestle was in first class condition and was well braced. The engine and train falling on the outside of the curve knocked down the outside post (batter post) and left the others standing. Eye witness[es] report that the train was approaching the trestle at the rate of 30 to 35 mph. The loss of life and personal injuries are very much regretted. The cause of the accident is being investigated. The trestle was promptly repaired and the first train passed over it at 9:10 this A.M. (Monday, September 28, 1903)*

The Mourning After

On the same day, the *Alexandria* [Virginia] *Gazette* incorrectly reported, in an article titled "Another Railroad Horror":

> *The trestle on which the wreck occurred was last night condemned by the officials of the road, and people were not allowed to come within 10 feet of it. It was in good condition when the wreck occurred, but the strain has made it dangerous. It is predicted that the entire structure will collapse before morning.*

Of course, by the time that news hit the streets, trains were already running over the trestle.

At 2:30 p.m. on Monday, a coroner's jury was assembled in Danville by acting coroner William A. Baugh in the Danville office of Constable F.M. Hamlin. The jurors were E.L. Gerst, W.S. Morison, M.F. Dove, B.T. Motley, C.E. Hughes and C.L. Booth. In three days of testimony, commonwealth attorney Thomas Hamlin intensely questioned, among others, E.H. Coapman, Southern Railway's Danville Division superintendent.

The verdict came down that

> *James T. Blair came to his death while in discharge of his duties as conductor on Train 97, by being caught in a wreck of the train No. 97… which train derailed on turning the curve near or on the Still House Trestle, said derailment caused by excessive speed of the train.*

Blair was the only casualty with Danville connections.

Even while the coroner's jury was meeting and trains were running over the newly repaired trestle, the wreckage was still in the process of being cleaned up. Southern officials allowed local people to take the wood from the demolished postal cars to their homes as firewood. Some, of course, took pieces of wood as souvenirs. John Wiley, however, decided against it. Wiley said:

> *I knowed it was a bad wreck when I seen it. Them cars were piled up so bad, torn up so bad they didn't move anything away but the iron. They gave the wood to people to use as firewood. I was just a young lad then. Nothing excited me. I didn't think about picking up no souvenirs.*

By Thursday, October 1, all the wreckage had been cleared, and Southern was in the process of removing the locomotive. The *Greensboro Record* for

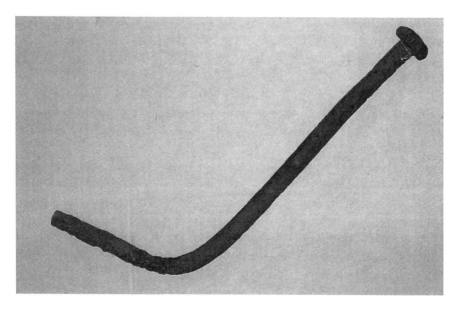

A nineteen-inch-long bolt found in the wreckage of Old 97. It may have been bent when the train's leap demolished wooden posts on Stillhouse Trestle. *Courtesy of Danville Museum of Fine Arts and History.*

October 5, 1903, reported, "The track has now been cleared entirely… Except for the new timbers in the trestle it is impossible to tell that a frightful disaster had recently occurred at the trestle."

According to Walter Seay, Southern Railway's yardmaster at Danville, locomotive No. 1102 was uprighted by a derrick from the train yard that was backed up on the trestle. A steel cable from it was attached to chains that had been pulled around the engine, and then the engine was set up on its drivers. A spur line from those tracks on the mill lot south of the trestle was extended up to the locomotive.

After the derrick was pushed down to that track by a switch engine, it lifted 1102 up to where its wheels came onto the new track. From there, engine 1102—minus its wooden cab, which had been pulverized in the wreck—was brought from the mill lot to the mainline track and hauled to Spencer, North Carolina, to be repaired.

W.D. Kizziah, a clerk of court at Salisbury, North Carolina, and son of a regular Old 97 engineer, Bill Kizziah of Spencer, told Raymond Carneal that when he was eight years old, engine 1102 was brought in from Danville, and it was still muddy. W.W. LeFabre, who worked in the Spencer shops, remembered when engine 1102 arrived there "wrapped in red mud."

The Mourning After

This photo is probably the most widely viewed of all the wreck scenes. It shows the uprighted engine several days after the wreck. The number 1102 appears on a circular plate on the front of the engine. Local residents had removed most of the wood from the wrecked cars. *Photo courtesy of Clara Fountain.*

During the days following the wreck, news spread along Old 97's Southern route and across the nation. On Monday afternoon, the day after the wreck, the *Danville Bee* came out with the headline "Horrible Railroad Catastrophe: Fast Mail Takes Fatal Plunge From Trestle." Not all the facts were known at that time, and some statements in the story were not accurate due to confusion about what had happened. Under these circumstances, the reporter had no choice but to use whatever information he had available.

Among the comments written in the *Bee* were the following:

> *The bodies of the dead men were broken almost entirely in pieces and horribly mangled, particularly about the head and face. The impact of the steam against the bodies of the engineer and fireman caused the skin and hair to fall away from their bodies. The scene itself baffles*

description. All the coaches are piled upon one another in the utmost confusion. All the cars except one are battered into kindling wood. The engine itself is buried in the mud at the bottom of the creek with the debris of the wreck piled high above it.

People living in the vicinity along either side of the track, many of whom were eye witnesses to the disaster, say that they were appalled at the rate of speed at which the train was running.

The article ended by stating that it was "one of the worst railroad wrecks that has taken place in Danville in many years."

Other newspapers followed in much the same vein, some repeating the *Bee* article. The *New York Times* for September 29 offered the headline: "A Train Falls 75 Feet, Everyone on Board Killed or Badly Injured, Cars and Cargo Demolished." The *Times* reported that the wreck happened while No. 97 was "running at a high rate of speed" and that the engine and cars were "reduced to a mass of twisted iron and steel and pieces of splintered wood." It included the charge that the engineer, Broady, was "unfamiliar with the road and didn't take into consideration the danger of coming onto the curve with such great velocity." The article concluded, "In loss of life this is one of the most serious wrecks that has occurred on the Southern."

The *New York Times* article illustrates how quickly misinformation spread after the wreck. Out of nineteen paragraphs, fifteen factual errors are evident, a number of which still persist to this day. Again, in all fairness to the *Times* writer, the rush to get out the news allowed little or no time for verifying information.

In the *Lynchburg News* for September 29, the headline read "Fast Mail Wrecked, Disastrous Accident on the Southern at Danville." Among its comments was the following:

It is said that the engineer on the doomed train was running a fast mail train for the first time. No. 97 is the fastest train on the road, and was coming into the city at the rate of between fifty and sixty miles an hour.

The Monday, September 28, edition of the *Richmond News Leader* ran a multilayered headline: "Nine Are Killed by Train's Wild Leap, Death and Destruction on the Rocks Below." The *Washington Post* headline for September 28 read: "Nine Fell to Death, Mail Train Plunged from Seventy-foot Trestle." A *Raleigh News and Observer* article for September 29 included the macabre title: "Death's Black Blank Swallowed Up Nine."

None of the articles had all the facts right because not all of the facts were known at that time. Newspapers were scrambling to notify their readers about the catastrophe.

In the days following the wreck, burials went on across Virginia and North Carolina. Joseph Broady was survived by his parents and George Broady, who had the sad duty of accompanying his brother's body to Saltville. Today, Joseph Andrew Broady's body rests at the Broady-Caywood Cemetery near Saltville. The marble gravestone reads, "Joseph A. Broady, Born April 1, 1870, Died September 27, 1903. 33 years 5 months and 26 days." He is buried near his father, David Broady, and his mother, Nancy Jane (Carpenter) Broady. Joseph Broady never married, but his fiancée, Ocie Ellen McCoy from Bluefield, West Virginia, reportedly attended his funeral.

Conductor John Thomas Blair was survived by his wife, the former Harriett Louise Bunger of Danville, and his children: five-year-old twin girls; a two-year-old daughter, Louise; and a baby three weeks old. Although the family lived in Spencer at the time, Harriett requested that he be buried in Danville. He was laid to rest at Green Hill Cemetery.

Flagman James Robert Moody of Raleigh left his wife, Hattie, and daughters, Edna Van Moody, age three, and Lois Irene Moody, born just a few months before April 6, 1903. Moody's body was sent to Raleigh on the afternoon of the twenty-eighth, escorted from Danville by members of the Brotherhood of Railroad Trainmen, Lodge No. 429, of Spencer, North Carolina. He was buried at Hayes Chapel Congregational Christian Church in Garner.

Albion G. "Buddy" Clapp, the fireman, who was engaged to Miss Mary Stanley, was buried at Springwood Presbyterian Church, about two miles south of Gibsonville, North Carolina. His tombstone reads, "Albion G. Clapp, Born Sept 9, 1870 Killed in Wreck No. 97 Danville, VA Sept 27, 1903." His fiancée, Miss Stanley, became principal of White Oak School in North Greensboro. She never married.

According to a local historian from Whitsett, North Carolina, when the family came to pick up Clapp's body, there was little left of him due to scalding by the steam. They just bundled up his remains in a sheet, took him back home and buried him the same day.

The body of apprentice fireman John Madison Hodge was sent to Raleigh, North Carolina, on Tuesday September 29. He was buried near the home of his parents with full military honors by the Raleigh Light Infantry. In the clerk's office of Wake County Superior Court is recorded the settlement by

Headstone of Old 97's engineer, Joseph A. Broady, near Saltville, Virginia. The inscription notes that he died on September 27, 1903.

the railroad. Southern paid $3,600 due to his death "in its railroad wreck near Danville, Virginia on September 27, 1903."

The *Rockingham Register* of Harrisonburg, Virginia, on October 2, 1903, covered the death of two of the postal clerks. Paul M. Argenbright, the former grade school principal, was survived by his father, Albert Argenbright, and also by his wife, the former Berta Miller, and a "child of tender age." He had been in the Railway Mail Service less than a year and had just returned from sick leave when he died in the wreck.

Postal clerk Daniel P. Flory was unmarried and was survived by his mother and his two brothers, who also worked for the Railway Mail Service. Flory had been a clerk for four or five years, and the article said of him that "he had the reputation of being a young man of the highest character and a most efficient postal clerk."

The *Washington Post* of September 28 reported that John L. Thompson of that city died in the wreck and was survived by his widow. He had just been promoted to a new position in July.

Of those mail clerks who survived, Charles E. Reames retired in 1930, and the others followed in later years. Percival Indermauer did not go back to the railroad but left the Railway Mail Service a year later, on September 21, 1904, on the eve of the wreck's anniversary. He transferred to the Washington city post office. Napoleon C. Maupin spent six months in the hospital with blood poisoning. He went to the transfer office at Union Station in Charlottesville and later became stationmaster. J. Harris Thompson was transferred to the "Valley run," Southern's line that ran between Harrisonburg, Lexington and Washington, D.C. Thompson died on March 4, 1963, and was buried at Stonewall Jackson Cemetery in Lexington.

Only mail clerks Frank G. Brooks and Jennings J. Dunlap returned to the Old 97 mail run. Brooks retired from Old 97 in 1919, and Dunlap worked the Washington–Charlotte mail route for thirty-eight years as clerk in charge of the mail car. Dunlap died on September 22, 1964, only days before the anniversary of the wreck. He was the last survivor of the wreck of Old 97.

In the days to come, the families of the dead went on with their lives, the wounded survivors regained their health and continued on with their jobs and the story eventually faded from the headlines. Yet the eyewitnesses could still picture the tragedy in their minds many years later. For one witness, however, the wreck made more than a lasting impression. Ruel Bullington, then a young boy, recalled the fear of trains he had from that day onward. In the *Danville Bee* of September 27, 1963, he said:

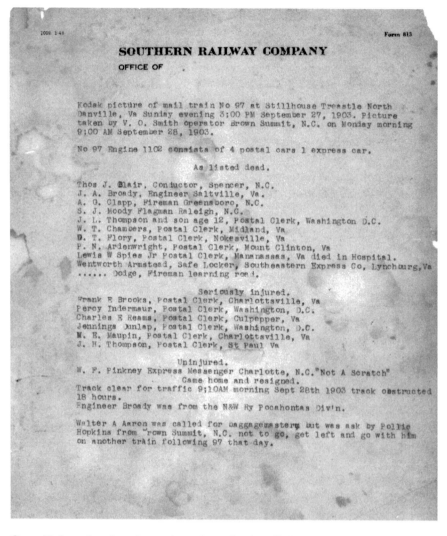

1000 1-46   Form 813

SOUTHERN RAILWAY COMPANY

OFFICE OF

Kodak picture of mail train No 97 at Stillhouse Treastle North
Danville, Va Sunday evening 3;00 PM September 27, 1903. Picture
taken by V. O. Smith operator Brown Summit, N.C. on Monday morning
9;00 AM September 28, 1903.

No 97 Engine 1102 consists of 4 postal cars 1 express car.

                    As listed dead.

Thos J. Blair, Conductor, Spencer, N.C.
J. A. Broady, Engineer Saltville, Va.
A. G. Clapp, Fireman Greensboro, N.C.
S. J. Moody Flagman Raleigh, N.C.
J. L. Thompson and son age 12, Postal Clerk, Washington D.C.
W. T. Chambers, Postal Clerk, Midland, Va
D. T. Flory, Postal Clerk, Nokesville, Va
P. N. Ardenwright, Postal Clerk, Mount Clinton, Va
Lewis W Spies Jr Postal Clerk, Mananassas, Va died in Hospital.
Wentworth Armstead, Safe Locker, Southeastern Express Co, Lynchburg,Va
...... Dodge, Fireman learning road.

                    Seriously injured.
Frank E Brooks, Postal Clerk, Charlottsville, Va
Percy Indermaur, Postal Clerk, Washington, D.C.
Charles E Reams, Postal Clerk, Culpepper, Va
Jennings Dunlap, Postal Clerk, Washington, D.C.
M. E. Maupin, Postal Clerk, Charlottsville, Va
J. H. Thompson, Postal Clerk, St Paul Va

                    Uninjured.
W. F. Pinkney Express Messenger Charlotte, N.C."Not A Scratch"
                    Came home and resigned.
Track clear for traffic 9;10AM morning Sept 28th 1903 track obstructed
18 hours.
Engineer Broady was from the N&W Ry Pocahontas Div'n.

Walter A Aaron was called for baggagemasterg but was ask by Pollie
Hopkins from "rown Summit, N.C. not to go, get left and go with him
on another train following 97 that day.

General information about the wreck typed on a Southern Railway stationery. The date is unknown, but it was evidently soon after the wreck since some of the "facts" listed are now known to be incorrect. *Photo courtesy of the Greensboro Chapter of the National Railway Historical Society.*

Some six or seven years [after the wreck] *we had moved across the river again—to the Cabell Street section. The Cabell Street Church—now Moseley Memorial—planned an outing for the kids. Finally they announced it would be a free train ride to Lynchburg and a chicken dinner there. It was free and I wanted some of that chicken. But I didn't go. I just couldn't force myself to ride a train across that trestle.*

The Mourning After

Despite the publicity this story received, at that time stories of railroad wrecks were as frequent as sawdust in a lumberyard. For that reason, the wreck of Old 97 did not seem destined to live on with any kind of permanence. However, this story did not die, and it did not fade away. Train 97 was fated to be wrecked again and again in the coming years, as court trials related to the catastrophe took place, including a decade-long legal battle over authorship of the ballad that arose from the wreck.

David Graves George from Franklin Junction, now Gretna, was on a train that arrived at the wreck probably the next day. He later claimed to have written a song that became a national hit, now known as "The Wreck of the Old 97." But George wasn't the only one there with an idea for a song. Fred Lewey, a native of Rockingham County, North Carolina, and a cousin of fireman Buddy Clapp, worked at the cotton mill nearby. He rushed out to help rescue survivors, likely realizing that Clapp was among those in the wreck. Lewey also claimed to have written the famous ballad.

BLAME IT ON GRAVITY

Sir Isaac Newton's law... That is what makes trains go downhill.
—Broady v. Southern Railway, *trial testimony, 1905*

All things considered, there is little doubt that speed can be blamed for the wreck of Old 97. Eyewitness testimony and that of postal clerk survivors presented earlier in this book confirm that the train was definitely running too fast as it approached the trestle. The coroner's jury convened the day after the wreck also concluded that "excessive speed" was the immediate cause of the tragedy. Yet, despite all that is known about the wreck of Old 97, we still don't know why Joseph "Steve" Broady did not slow the train down when he reached Stillhouse Trestle.

From the beginning, Joseph Broady alone has been blamed for the accident. Freeman Hubbard, in *Railroad Avenue*, wrote:

> *Everybody involved seemed to have a satisfactory alibi—that is, everybody but Joe Broady. Consequently, blame for the tragedy was heaped upon the dead engineer who made the mistake of running the train as fast as he could.*

Unfortunately, during that time errors crept into news reports, and over the years speculation about what happened has been treated as fact. In addition, a lot of what is believed about the train wreck comes from the ballad "The Wreck of the Old 97," which tells a story but is not necessarily accurate history.

The common view that Joseph Broady was reckless and irresponsible in running the train doesn't seem to be totally true. Trial testimony previously presented in the text supports that conclusion. Postal clerk survivors indicated that Joe Broady was going very fast in some places between Monroe and Danville but not all the time. Some indicated that he ran the train at about the usual speed. Southern's Danville Division superintendent, E.H. Coapman, stated that Broady had made up only two minutes from Monroe to Fall Creek Station, which is about six miles out of Danville. Coapman also testified that on other regular runs Old 97 had made faster time than that.

Regardless of how Broady ran the train from Lynchburg to Danville, Old 97 did fail to slow down when it reached the warning sign a short distance above the trestle. Southern Railway had recognized that it was a dangerous trestle, thus a fifteen-mile-per-hour speed limit was imposed on trains going over it. In a final statement to the court during the 1905 trial, Southern noted that "this track and trestle, with the same grade, and curves, and without guard rails, had been in constant and daily use for thirty years, without an accident, proving…its safety, and suitability for the uses to which it was put."

It makes no sense to believe that Joe Broady *attempted* to cross the trestle at excessive speed, since he had spoken of how dangerous it was and had also brought trains across there at least two dozen times before the wreck—all obviously at appropriate speeds. Pat Fox offers further insight:

> *Why hadn't Joe Broady slowed the express down? He knew he had to go very slowly across the trestle in a sharp turn, move cautiously downriver for half a mile and then make a still sharper turn onto the railroad bridge over Dan River. Even if he could have made speed past these critical points, he had to take his second scheduled stop* [the first one being Lynchburg] *at the station just beyond the river.*

There is no evidence that Broady purposely attempted the trestle at an unsafe speed.

It has been suggested that Broady's unfamiliarity with the route caused him to forget where the trestle was. Yet, it has been established that Broady knew the road and therefore must have known where the trestle was located. Perhaps it was the fact that he *did know* where the trestle was that created the problem that led to the fatal accident.

In my interview with Louis Newton—a retired railroad official for Norfolk and Western and later Norfolk Southern Railways whose knowledge of those railroads is said to be both encyclopedic and legendary—Newton advanced the idea that the trains Broady ran for Southern before Old 97 were all freight trains, and probably most, if not all, those that Broady ran at Norfolk and Western in the coalfields years earlier were freight trains as well. Running Old 97 for the first time, Broady would have experienced a much lighter train with fewer cars. He wasn't used to the ease of operation; it made him overconfident, and he overreached himself. When Broady approached the trestle, perhaps he thought he could easily slow down, but it didn't happen.

This view concurs with that of Terry Feichtenbiner, a longtime certified locomotive engineer and road foreman of engines for the C&O Railway, who has had a lifetime of experience running both freight and passenger trains, with considerable time in special train movements involving steam locomotives. In my interview with him, he explained how Broady's lack of experience on short trains with only a handful of cars could have failed him.

Feichtenbiner notes that a major difference in braking power exists between a four-car passenger train (as Old 97 was classified) going sixty miles per hour on level ground compared to a freight train of fifty cars at the same speed. The same braking application that would slow down the longer, heavier freight train would make no noticeable difference on the four-car train. Fifty cars would be braking simultaneously on the longer train, whereas the shorter train would have only four cars braking together. The more cars, the more brakes to slow the train down.

Feichtenbiner concludes:

> *Thus, a short passenger train such as Broady was handling required a much larger brake application to reduce its speed. As Broady was descending the grade toward the 15 MPH speed restriction* [at the trestle], *it is possible that he allowed his speed to become too great, and waited until he was too close to the curve in order for the available braking power to overcome the speed.*

The most prevalent theory about why the train wrecked was that Broady was "whittling" all along the route; that is, heavy braking multiple times in close succession without allowing time for the air reservoirs on each car to be resupplied before the train brakes were applied again. Coming on the downgrade from Lima to the trestle would have taken just a few minutes, but if he had "lost his airbrakes," as the ballad says, then Joe Broady would have been the engineer of a train out of control.

Postal clerks testified in the trial that they did not notice the train "checking up" until it got to the trestle. It stands to reason that the postal clerks would have been standing up sorting the mail and would have noticed the slightest application of the train's brakes, especially if Broady had been back and forth on the brakes. However, the mail clerks may not have meant that he never braked but that he kept the train at a fast speed continually.

It seems unbelievable that Broady would not have used his brakes between Lynchburg and Danville. As previously noted, Dave Stephenson's studies on the power of engine 1102 pulling just four cars, the train could easily go up and down the grades between Monroe and Danville without any struggle at all. Going uphill would not have been a problem, but going very fast downhill, especially with curves in the track, would have necessitated using the brakes to some degree. So "whittling" was quite likely part of the problem if Broady was trying to make up time.

Raymond Carneal, in his history of the wreck, argues that engine 1102's steam pump was powerful enough to recharge the brake line with air quickly, even with more cars than Broady's locomotive pulled. Thus, regardless of how Broady ran the train, losing his airbrakes would not have been the problem. Terry Feichtenbiner challenges that notion, stressing that air reservoirs have specific recharging times, since only a certain amount of air can be pumped through the brake line at one time. Having a highly efficient steam pump doesn't make that happen any quicker.

Feichtenbiner also adds:

> In the worst case possible, if the reservoirs are depleted severely enough, the brakes on the cars will not apply at all, even with an emergency brake application made by the engineer placing his train brake valve handle into the "big hole," or emergency position. With steam locomotives, when the train brakes fail to slow the train, or to even apply, the engineer has only his locomotive independent brake remaining for use, and at high speed, it is of little significance. The independent brake can be operated "independent" of the train brakes, thus the name, and its extent is limited to the brakes on the wheels of the locomotive and tender only. In this scenario, it would be likely that Broady's last resort was his independent brake, and he probably used every bit he had.

Whether Broady was overconfident about the distance needed to slow the train down before he reached the trestle or whether he realized he had "lost his air" due to over use of the brakes, either situation could have led to panic. Maybe that explains the continuous screaming whistle that got folks' attention as the train approached the trestle. Stopping a train is not as simple as pushing in the brake pedal on an automobile. With a steam locomotive, it is a process involving valves and levers, so it is not instantaneous and requires an engineer to focus—harder to do in a panic.

Bob Miller, a retired Chesapeake and Ohio conductor, suggests an additional possibility. After shutting off the throttle and "dumping the air" to apply the brakes, only to find them useless, Broady might have attempted to put the train into reverse. The Johnson, or reverse, bar took much effort to engage. Once that was done, the throttle would be opened back up to pull the engine backward. That process takes more than a few seconds.

Either scenario—throwing the train into emergency; that is, "big-holing" the engine, which means to apply the brakes heavily by releasing all the air in the brake line at once or, after doing so, attempting to reverse the wheels— could explain the accident. Howard Gregory explained:

> *If the airbrakes of a locomotive are thrown into emergency on a curve, there is a tendency for the engine boiler to lift off the frame and wheels, allowing the flanges of the wheels to raise up enough to ride over the rail. If the flange fails to clear the top of the rail, the terrific pressure exerted against the outside rail could cause it to pull the spikes loose from the ties and turn over, thus ensuring a derailment.*

Evidence from the 1905 trial supports Gregory's comment because the right drivers jumped the track and bumped along the ties with the left drivers raised off the track.

If Broady threw the train into emergency, there would be other serious consequences. After applying the brakes heavily, the cast-iron brake shoes would have rapidly overheated. That could explain the sparks that at least one eyewitness saw and the loud noise heard right before the wreck.

But there was a more serious consequence than overheated brakes. Bob Miller, in examining a photograph of the engine on its side, pointed out that a tire was missing from the middle driver or wheel on the exposed side. Tires are wide metal bands that are heated and then allowed to cool around the wheels, causing the metal to contract and tighten. Terry Feichtenbiner expressed to me that braking heavily or reversing the wheels would generate intense heat immediately, and the tires would have heated up and expanded enough to come off. If so, a loose tire would have derailed the engine.

Whatever Joe Broady did to slow the train was too little, too late. Perhaps some mechanical failure was at fault, but the locomotive was said to be in perfect condition when it left Monroe.

The trestle, looking toward the south. Photo by John Wilson, a longtime Danville policeman and avid photographer. The markings on the picture are his, with an "X" to show where Old 97 left the track. His daughter, Dolores Reynolds of Danville, found this photo among his files sometime after his death.

Regardless, what we do know is that once the speeding train left the trestle and sailed into space, the laws of physics regarding momentum and centrifugal force came into play. Ultimately, gravity put it on the ground. Sunday, September 27, 1903, was a big day for Isaac Newton's laws of motion but a bad day for Old 97 and its crew.

As previously stated in trial testimony, the train derailed about fifty feet before it reached the trestle, the right drivers bumping along the crossties, with the left wheels likely in the air. About thirty-five to forty feet onto the trestle, the train launched into the ravine, damaging rails, ties and wooden posts as it went over.

The trestle was elevated three and a half inches on the western, or right, side—the side the train went over. Semmens and Goldfinch, in *How Steam Locomotives Really Work*, stated that the cant or elevation on one side of a curve is

fixed by the geometry of the track and is therefore correct at one speed. If this speed is exceeded there will be a sideways force exerted by the flanges.

128

Blame It on Gravity

Up to a point this is acceptable, but if it becomes greater than the rail fastenings can stand, it will "burst the track," with disastrous results.

Railroad officials at the 1905 trial, while testifying that the required speed for Stillhouse Trestle was fifteen miles an hour, admitted that the train should still have been able to negotiate the curve at twenty-five miles per hour. Broady and Old 97 had to have been going faster than that.

The general consensus by those on the ground and those inside the cars who claimed to be adept at figuring train speeds suggests that the train's speed on the trestle was close to sixty miles an hour. But how fast was it really going when it left the trestle?

Two mechanical engineering students at Virginia Tech took on the challenge to determine the speed of Old 97 when it left the trestle. Preston Stoakes, a doctoral engineering candidate, and John Meier, a rising senior, both worked on the problem using particle dynamics formulas, which analyze particle motion in order to provide a conservative estimate of the train's speed.

After being provided with the pertinent facts necessary for their calculations, both engineers, using slightly different numbers, came up with similar estimates. If the engine left the trestle on a straight line consistent with Newton's laws of motion, and if the locomotive landed where it came to rest, 213 feet away, then it was traveling at least eighty (Meier) or eighty-four (Stoakes) miles per hour.

Trial testimony indicated that the cars may have landed about 50 feet behind the locomotive. Preston Stoakes calculated that if the engine landed 163 feet away from where it left the trestle, or where the cars landed, and came to rest at the place indicated, then the speed coming off the trestle was about sixty-five miles per hour.

Using a topographic map showing the tangent line where the train left the track and continued onward indicates that the locomotive might have hit the middle of the bank right below the mill building and rebounded to where it came to rest. Stoakes estimated that if the train hit the bank and rebounded twenty-five feet, as Danville Division superintendent E.H. Coapman testified, then it would have left the trestle at seventy-five miles per hour.

Steam locomotives also have high centers of gravity. As part of the analysis by Virginia Tech engineers, the rollover speed of engine 1102 on the elevated track with a ten-degree curve was determined using centrifugal force calculations. Preston Stoakes concluded:

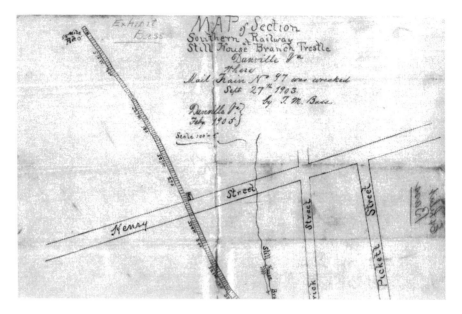

This map by local surveyor T.M. Bass features "Still House Branch Trestle," where Old 97 wrecked. It was prepared in 1905 and was used as evidence in the civil trial *Estate of Joseph Broady v. Southern Railway*.

The train should roll over at about 60 mph but wouldn't jump the track until a much higher speed. This is consistent with the testimony that the train rode on the right wheels until it hit the bridge. I believe it would also indicate the rails were worn, making it easier for it to jump.

These conclusions verify information presented in the 1905 trial. It was argued that the rails were worn, although it was denied by Southern that this had anything to do with the wreck.

In the final analysis, the best conclusion is that Old 97 left the track at speeds between sixty-five and eighty-five miles per hour, with the actual speed being about seventy-five miles per hour if one goes by Coapman's testimony and the supposition that the locomotive probably made impact with the bank at the mill building corner.

The high speeds calculated by Stoakes and Meier verify eyewitness accounts previously mentioned. It appears that Old 97 was not just going fast, but very fast. Jessie Giles said that Old 97 "came by us ps-s-s-shew, just coming like a bullet...like a puff of wind...It was out of control, no doubt about that...He could have been going 90 all right." Eyewitness John Wiley said it was going "so fast you didn't have time to wink your eyes before it hit the trestle."

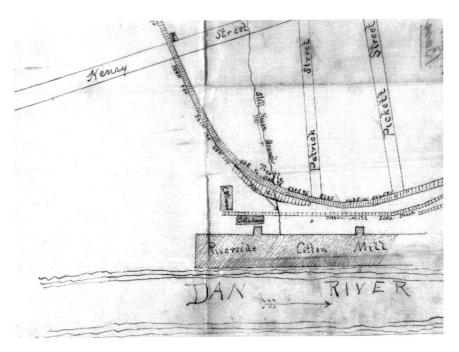

Features of the Bass map include streets around the trestle and the location of Riverside Cotton Mill buildings. Degree coordinates for the curve are marked along the track, and an arrow shows that the locomotive landed 213 feet from the north end of the trestle.

These confirmations of the fast speed of the train and a study of other factors that entered into the wreck of Old 97 still do not tell us exactly why it happened. The only person who could do that is Joseph Andrew Broady, who never lived to tell his story.

Why Broady ran the train so fast at the trestle and at other times is important because it reflects on Joseph Broady's character—the kind of man he was—and how that influenced the decisions he might have made during those final moments. He has been labeled a boomer engineer, floating from job to job because of violations of the rules or because he had a restless nature, but I am not aware of any significant evidence to support that theory. Joseph Broady had a fine reputation as a person and as an engineer, and he knew the danger of the trestle. Whatever happened on Sunday, September 27, 1903, does not necessary mean he suddenly became irresponsible or became desperate to prove his worth.

Perhaps no one else was available when Broady was assigned to Old 97, but Broady's lack of experience on a lighter, faster train than he was used to may have been the determining factor in what happened. Terry Feichenbiner

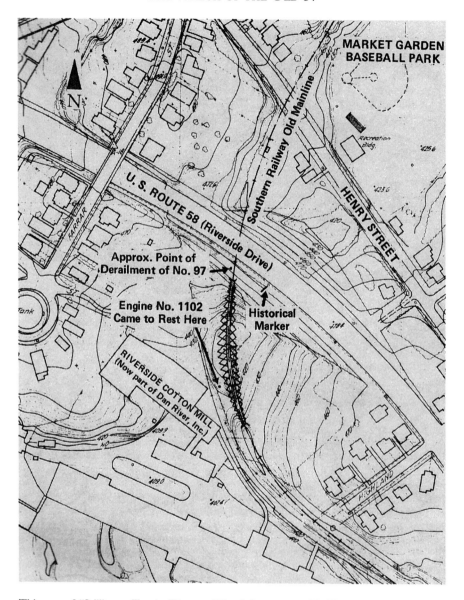

This map of "Stillhouse Trestle: Then and Now" first appeared in Howard Gregory's history of the wreck. *Prepared by City of Danville Engineering Department.*

summed up the problem for Broady in that regard: "Familiarity with the road is important, but the engineer must understand how his equipment is going to react to the road, and to the engineer's actions." In short, it is conceivable that Broady knew the road but just didn't know the train.

In addition, with Old 97 also arriving late in Monroe, Broady was likely thrust into a situation he had not anticipated, a situation that prompted this newly hired extra engineer to attempt to make up more than just a little time on an unfamiliar train. He had no choice but to do his best, and he failed.

Broady's train was definitely going too fast for the trestle, but in my estimation, Joseph Broady cannot be faulted for not knowing the train he was asked to run for the first time on September 27, 1903, especially since that train was behind schedule. Besides, Conductor Blair, who was in charge of the train, had every right to signal Broady to slow down if he was running the train too fast, and Broady would have been obligated to do so according to railroad rules.

Broady no doubt made mistakes in handling Old 97, maybe due to overconfidence or perhaps out of frustration with being behind schedule and confronted with slow orders, run-late orders and other hindrances to making up time. Sadly, we'll never know for sure what actually transpired that day with Joe Broady and Old 97. So the legend continues.

OLD 97 OVER THE YEARS

Into the twilight of truth and legend.
—Danville Bee, *September 1953*

Not all of the news related to the wreck of Old 97 was bad. There were some happy endings. Earl Nostrandt, who was playing marbles with his friends that day on Myrtle Avenue and stood near the north side of the trestle peering at the destruction, later met Myrtle Poole, the little girl who rode the trolley and stood with her family at the south end of the trestle. They were married, not because of the wreck of Old 97, but they did share their memories of being on opposite ends of the trestle that day.

Clarence Goodloe, the mail clerk on the Washington–Chicago route who sometimes rode Old 97 down to Danville to see his girlfriend of eighteen years, finally tied the knot because of the wreck. In an interview with his grandson, Barney Lawless, Lawless told me that Goodloe's girlfriend saw the wreck as an omen that they should be married. Both were in their forties, and they married that October.

Among other things, engine 1102 was put back in service, but as far as anyone knows, it never again pulled Old 97. For years, it pulled trains from Richmond to Danville and then from Greensboro to Goldsboro, North Carolina. The famous engine ended its career in East St. Louis, where, in 1929, it made one last hurrah under engineer W.Z. Knight, setting a one-month fuel record. After a long career, it was sent to the scrap yard at

Princeton, Indiana. The *Indianapolis News* for Saturday, November 18, 1933, reported that only a rusty boiler and one driving wheel remained at the time.

The Fast Mail service continued, with train 97 running the mail route from Washington to Atlanta as usual. Unfortunately, Congress discontinued the post office contract after 1907 because a financial panic that year caused the New York Stock Exchange to fall 50 percent, and many state and local banks and businesses declared bankruptcy.

George Broady, engineer Joseph Broady's brother, worked for Southern Railway at the time of the wreck and continued in its service. He retired as road foreman of engines after fifty years. George moved to Saltville after retirement but was buried in Spencer, North Carolina.

Southern Railway made financial settlements with the various families of those killed in the wreck. Among them, court records in Danville, Virginia, indicate that a jury awarded mail clerk John L. Thompson's estate $8,000 on April 28, 1904, and on another day, the estate of Paul M. Argenbright was awarded $6,000.

Joseph Broady's estate claim was challenged. Testimony has been included throughout this book from the civil trial that followed in July 1905, when the Broady estate sued the Southern Railway. The trial took place in Danville, Virginia, with Judge A.M. Aiken presiding. Testimony came from railroad officials, local citizens, survivors of the wreck, eyewitnesses and experts of all sorts on matters of railroading.

In *Estate of Joseph Broady v. Southern Railway*, the plaintiff attorneys basically accused the railroad of having an unsafe trestle. However, at the end of the trial, Southern Railway's attorneys contributed the following statement in its final argument:

> *We respectfully submit that a careful review of the testimony in this case will show that the death of Joseph A. Broady was caused by his own want of care and recklessness... The fact remains that the blame for this fearful disaster must rest with him, and there can be no recovery in this action.*

The jury, however, sided with the plaintiff and awarded Broady's estate $4,500 instead of the $10,000 requested.

By 1916, the court cases related to the wreck were in the distant past, and Southern continued on with its efforts to improve the track that Old 97 ran on. The mainline that Old 97 traveled from Lynchburg to Danville was double tracked and rerouted, with the necessary upgrades included. It split off from the old track's path at the base of White Oak Mountain near State Road 863, just off highway Route 29. Southern Railway received permission

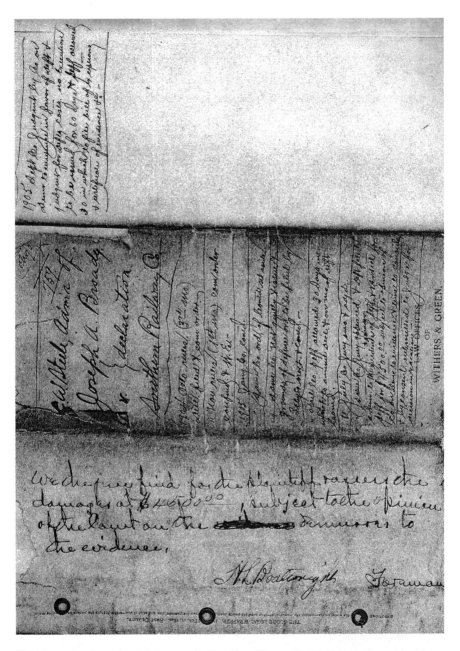

This document from the circuit court clerk's office of Danville, Virginia, indicates that the jury awarded Joseph Broady's estate $4,500 in the July 1905 trial against Southern Railway.

Southern Railway Mail and Express train No. 97, with engineer Joseph A. "Steve" Broady at the throttle. *Painting by H.L. Cocke, Blairs, Virginia.*

The Danville railroad depot, 1912. This station was the next scheduled stop after No. 97 left Lynchburg. Notice the car, horse-and-buggies and locomotive all in one picture. *Photo courtesy of Lawrence McFall.*

This historical marker, placed in 1947 on Route 58 at the scene of the wreck of Old 97, lists the total fatalities incorrectly as nine instead of the actual number of eleven.

from the ICC to abandon that portion of the old mainline from Fall Creek right outside of Danville to Lima in 1925, and the portion from Lima down to the trestle was approved for abandonment in 1935. The trestle, along with the track, was removed at some point afterward, but portions of the original track bed with culverts can still be seen below White Oak Mountain and on into Danville.

The route from White Oak Mountain now travels east of where it used to go and passes under the railroad bridge on Route 29 at Blairs, Virginia,

Aerial view of the trestle area in March 2010, with a line superimposed over the image to show the path of track through the curve of the trestle and an "X" to show the location where engine 1102 landed. *Photo courtesy of Hutch Hutcheson of Virginia MultiMedia.*

a mile or so from White Oak Mountain. The present track continues on toward Danville and enters the railroad station from a bridge downstream of the original bridge that crossed the Dan River on September 27, 1903.

A lot of the ravine that the trestle crossed was filled in for a highway project bringing Route 58, which runs east to west across the bottom of the state, through Danville. The road is now known as Riverside Drive as it passes through the city toward Martinsville. A state highway marker stands on that road near the site where the train jumped the trestle. It reports that nine were killed instead of the correct number of eleven.

A deep cut off the road below the historical marker, once part of the ravine, is now filled with trees and vegetation. The Riverside Cotton Mill buildings, known as the Long Mill, burned down in 2008, but Stillhouse Creek still runs through the site into the Dan River. The site can be viewed along the Riverwalk Trail in Danville from the entrance near Union Street Bridge off Riverside Drive.

At Fall Creek, where Old 97 passed on its way to destruction, the railroad station was converted into a restaurant in later years and named the Old 97 Steak House. A local motorcycle shop in Danville goes by the name Old 97 Choppers.

Above: The Old 97 mural by artist Wes Hardin in downtown Danville, Virginia, at the intersection of Memorial Drive and Main Street.

Right: This scale model of the wreck site by John Duncan is on display in the railroad station building at the Danville Science Center, located off Craghead Street in Danville, Virginia.

This children's book on the wreck of Old 97 was published by Clara Fountain in 1976. Students at Grove Park Elementary School in Danville prepared the illustrations. The cover illustration was by her son, Marc Fountain.

Old 97 Over the Years

Each year, the Danville Science Center, which is partly located in the present Amtrak train station, sponsors Rail Days on the weekend closest to the wreck anniversary. In the wreck's centennial year, 2003, the Danville Science Center, the Danville Museum of Fine Arts and History and the AAF Tank Museum sponsored a number of activities to celebrate the 100th anniversary of the wreck, which included a scaled-down model train exhibit, a concert with bluegrass star Ricky Skaggs and local singing sensation Janette Williams, a Pullman's Ball and a tour of the wreck sites, among other events.

Artistic endeavors on different levels have turned to the wreck of Old 97 for inspiration. The Danville Science Center on Craghead Street in downtown Danville displays the scale model of the trestle by John Duncan depicting the wreck scene. The model, made to meticulous specifications over a period of two and a half years, is accompanied by wood that came from the original trestle. Also in the downtown area, a gigantic mural by Wes Hardin depicting the wreck graces the side of a building near the intersection of Main Street and Memorial Drive.

Clara Fountain, a librarian in the Danville public schools, wrote the first children's book about the tragedy, *The Wreck of the Old 97*, in 1976 and had students illustrate it with drawings. Danny Ricketts, a local historian, and his wife, Nancye, produced *The Wreck of the Old 97* coloring book in 2003, also the first of its kind.

Although some local artists have painted renditions of the wreck, the famous midwestern artist Thomas Hart Benton painted a symbolic work titled *The Wreck of Old 97*. Not meant to be a portrayal of the actual wreck, it demonstrates the Industrial Age confrontation between horse and wagon and train. The work shows the awe of man toward the machine while at the same time contrasting an older way of life with a newer one. Even the landscape featured in the painting tends to sway with the tension.

The story of Old 97 has also appeared in other settings. During World War II, Japanese propagandist Tokyo Rose told the GIs over the radio that she would play them something that would make them homesick: "The Wreck of the Old 97." On the other end of the spectrum, the *Danville Register* ran a nationally syndicated *Dennis the Menace* cartoon in 1991 titled "Choo-Choo Man," which mentioned the Old 97, adding a little humor to an otherwise sad tale.

Movies, too, have gotten into the act of Old 97, especially the song. The 1932 Hollywood film *Scarface* has a woman at a piano singing the ballad. In the movie *Blues Brothers*, while the band is preparing to leave after performing at a country nightclub, Elwood apologized about a list

An original wax cylinder belonging to David Luther featuring Vernon Dalhart's 1924 recording of "The Wreck on the Southern Old 97" for Edison Talking Machine Company.

of songs they were expected to play, saying, "Sorry we couldn't remember 'The Wreck of Old 97.'"

That famous song, of course, is the greatest legacy of the wreck. In 1924, the song, originally titled "The Wreck on the Southern Old 97," was recorded by Vernon Dalhart first for Edison and then for Victor Talking Machine Company. Thereafter, the Southern mountain ballad reached national prominence and became the first song to sell over a million records. Danville historian Kinney Rorrer, an authority on old-time music, notes that the flip side featured "The Prisoner's Song," but it never reached the popularity of "Old 97." Dalhart's recording changed the music industry. As Rorrer said, "It put country music in business."

Since then, "The Wreck of the Old 97"—both story and song—has continued to grow in popularity and spread across the globe. Rorrer, who took a college class on a tour group of Scotland a few years ago, noted that a customs agent there took special note of the passport of one of his students, Patrick Touart, and remarked, "Danville, Virginia. That's where the Old 97 went down!"

The song has been recorded by scores of musicians covering a wide range of music genres. The list is long, but a few familiar names are Mac Wiseman, Lester Flatt and Earl Scruggs, the Statler Brothers (their first recording), Hank Snow, Boxcar Willie, Roy Acuff, Woody Guthrie, Eddie Arnold, Johnny Mercer, Kate Smith, Danny Kay, Pete Seeger, Hank Williams III and Johnny Cash.

Besides country and folk versions, there have been jazz and Big Band versions also. A current Texas country rock band called the Old 97s took its name from the wreck of the Old 97. Two of the band's albums are titled *Wreck that Train* and *Blame It on Gravity*.

The song's popularity can be attributed to the resounding success of the Dalhart version, which was based on a record by Henry Whitter, a local singer around Fries, Virginia. Whitter's lyrics can be traced to an original version by Fred Lewey and Charles Noell. Whitter's version follows:

THE WRECK OF THE OLD 97
(The Wreck on the Southern Old 97)

They gave him his orders at Monroe, Virginia,
Saying Steve you're way behind time.
This is not "Thirty-Eight" but it's "Old Ninety-Seven"
You must put her in Spencer on time.

Steve Brooklyn said to his black greasy fireman,
Just shovel on a little more coal,
And when we cross that White Oak Mountain,
You can watch old Ninety-Seven roll.

It's a mighty rough road from Lynchburg to Danville,
And a line on a three-mile grade.
It was on this grade that he lost his airbrakes
And you see what a jump he made.

He was going down grade making ninety miles an hour
When his whistle began to scream,

Sheet music featuring "The Wreck on the Southern Old 97" by Henry Whitter. Published in New York by Triangle Music Publishing Co. *Courtesy of Kinny Rorrer.*

He was found in the wreck with his hand on the throttle
And was scalded to death by steam.

So come you ladies you must take warning
From this time, now and on,
Never speak harsh words to your true loving husband,
He may leave you and never return.

A folksong like "The Wreck of the Old 97" gets changed a lot as it is passed along by oral tradition, which produces many versions. Other versions, including Johnny Cash's first version, departs from the one above, but even so, Whitter's version is the basis for most modern-day renditions.

David Graves George and his wife, Marie Murphy, on September 10, 1944. George claimed to have written "The Wreck of the Old 97," but his claim was eventually rejected by a federal court of appeals, as well as the United States Supreme Court. He died in 1948. *Photo courtesy of Manuscripts Print Collection, Special Collections Library, University of Virginia.*

As an example of how musicians change lyrics to suit their taste, David Luther, a former Danville radio personality whose grandfather remembered the actual Old 97 wreck, recalled being in Nashville at a country music convention to which deejays from around the nation were invited. Johnny Cash was there and explained to Luther why he changed the phrase "black greasy fireman" in his first recording of the song to "big greasy fireman." It was in the late '60s, during the time of the civil rights movement, and Cash told Luther he did not want to upset anyone with the words.

The fact that different versions of the song appeared early in folk tradition is partly responsible for a legal battle that led to the ballad becoming the first song copyright case to reach the United States Supreme Court.

After Dalhart's version brought national popularity to the ballad, a claimant to authorship appeared—David Graves George of Pittsylvania County, Virginia, the telegraph operator at the Gretna station when Old 97 passed by. He claimed to have visited the wreck site the next day and, in a few weeks or a month, wrote the words to the song. He said he put it to the melody of "The Ship that Never Returned" because, as a friend at a barbershop suggested, "It's a right purty tune."

After reading that Victor Talking Machine Company was seeking the author of the ballad to award royalties, George published a suspicious letter in the *Richmond News Leader* in 1927, stating, "I with others wrote the poetry of 97." He then requested the letter back and changed the words to read, "I alone." George attempted to negotiate with Victor, which had already settled with Lewey and Noell, so he received no satisfaction concerning royalties from the use of *his* song. In turn, he sued the company for damages.

The trial took place in the Federal District Court of New Jersey. There, George's case was weakened by his own testimony, especially in light of the *News Leader* letter; suspicious agreement between witnesses, including friends and family; discrepancies in evidence he presented as fact; comments from at least one person whose testimony George "attempted" to manipulate; plus the testimony of a folklore expert from Harvard, Robert Gordon, and the testimony of an expert in handwriting and chemical analysis.

When all was said and done, despite the preponderance of evidence against George, Judge Avis, on March 31, 1933, ruled that he was sure beyond a "moral certainty" that George was the true author of the ballad. He ignored or explained away the expert witness testimony, stating that they "erred in their conclusions."

When Victor appealed this decision, it came before the Third Circuit Court of Appeals at Philadelphia in January 1934. That court voted unanimously to reverse the district court ruling. Circuit judge J. Warren Davis wrote the appeal court's opinion, pointing out the weaknesses of the plaintiff's case. He stated:

> *It is established beyond doubt that Lewey and Noell wrote the songs bearing their names…The plaintiff's witnesses do not satisfy us that he wrote the song, and the documentary evidence so discredits his testimony as to lead us to the conclusion that he has not borne the burden the law casts upon him. His position was not strengthened, but rather weakened by the evidence of the defendant* [Victor].

After this ruling, George's attorney appealed the case to the United States Supreme Court, arguing that Victor had gone beyond the time limit in appealing to the Third Circuit. On December 17, 1934, the U.S. Supreme Court agreed, ruling that the initial decision had not been final, and sent the case back to the district court. The district court's decision was then reinstated, and Victor was required to present evidence related to the amount of damages the company would have to pay. On September 15, 1938, the district court awarded George $65,295.56 as his financial settlement.

The story did not end there. Victor appealed again to the Third Circuit Court of Appeals, which saw no reason to change its first decision, so it again reversed the district court ruling and settlement. When George appealed to the U.S. Supreme Court again, the court refused to hear the case and let the appeals court decision stand. A second petition for a rehearing was also denied by the Supreme Court on January 29, 1940, thus ending over a decade of legal battles. George received not a cent for his trouble, whereas Lewey and Noell, who had both previously received a small compensation from Victor, never pursued the issue further.

In the *Journal of American Folklore* article "Robert Gordon and the second Wreck of 'Old 97,'" Norm Cohen offers the following conclusion to George's claim:

> *I am tempted to give credence to George's claim of authorship of a ballad about a train wreck…a ballad that was in circulation for a while…but later even he forgot it; so that when he heard the Dalhart record, he knew he had written something about Old 97 and concluded that Dalhart's song was his ballad. The rest was simply a matter of buttressing what he knew as a weak, though just, case…The alternative to this explanation, of course, is that George fabricated the entire story.*

David George died in 1948, but the controversy continues to this day. On September 28, 1966, the *Gazette-Virginian* of South Boston, Virginia, published a letter to the editor from George's son, David Gordon George. He took issue with a disparaging commentary about his father published in that paper. The son stated that his father's authorship was

> *acknowledged by more than 30 publications of record, sheet music, etc and that virtually all of these paid him sums ranging from hundreds to thousands of dollars, during a period from six to ten years after the first litigation was first instituted in 1928. My father fought tenaciously to the bitter end and, throwing into this unequal struggle, all that he had collected from the other companies, and gave up only when the costs of further effort became prohibitive.*

His son further noted that his father had collected more than thirty statements from people of all walks of life, including a considerable number of railroad people. They were "from good, solid, respected citizens who clearly recalled and unhesitatingly asserted that my father was author."

One regret David Gordon George had was that at some point in the legal battle his father should have accepted a $50,000 offer Victor made to settle. His father would not do it, stating, "I'll live on wild onions before I accept that amount from them."

What did David Graves George write if not "The Wreck of the Old 97"? Kinny Rorrer said, "I believe David George wrote something, perhaps about another wreck he confused with Old 97 in later years." Whatever the truth, David George's name will always be associated with "The Wreck of the Old 97" as the following poem, from a newspaper account, so amiably recites:

> *A train, wrecked thirty years ago,*
> *Now brings immortal fame,*
> *Not only to a number, but*
> *To David George's name.*
> *For now, "Old 97's Wreck,"*
> *This David George contends,*
> *Was written by himself, and he*
> *Should share its dividends.*
>
> *And thus the tragedies of life*
> *Oft prove a benefit,*
> *For poor Old 97's crash*
> *Became a record hit.*
>
> *The record makers long declined*
> *Its profits to disgorge*
> *'Til David proved in federal court*
> *The song was his, by George!*

Near the end of his legal crusade, George found sympathy in a *Danville Commercial Appeal* article (written sometime after 1938) titled "Ballad of Old 97...Woeful Song of Historic Wreck Causes Tragedy." Writer Valerie Nicholson alleged:

> *The story that follows is almost as sad as the wreck—maybe even sadder, for it deals with the raising of a man's hopes and the wrecking of them, time and again, and the sort of legal battle that, stretched out*

over years and years, embitters the very depths of a man's soul. It's an
open question as to whether it's better to be scalded to death by steam,
quickly, or have your spirit battered around in years of legal tussling,
Recognition Refused.

To many, it may have appeared that the legal drama was a classic matchup between a modern-day David and Goliath—a poor Virginia farmer with a large family up against a national corporation with powerful influence and deep pockets—in this case, Victor Talking Machine Company.

As usual, the truth about the song, as well as what actually happened on September 27, 1903, is more complex than tradition has us believe. Today, despite the confusion and controversies surrounding Old 97 found in both story and song, the legend lives on, a concoction of fact and fiction.

As if to prove that the story is destined to remain with us, on September 26, 1966, Pat Fox filed a story with United Press International, stating, "Yesterday, at about 1:30 p.m., Robert Burns George, 78, of Gretna, VA, was killed by Train Number 21 as it passed through town. Number 21 replaced famed Mail Train 97 on its run from Washington, D.C. to Atlanta." Fox wrote that Robert Burns George had been walking along the track that day—the day before the Old 97 wreck anniversary. And not only was he killed in the hometown of David George, who claimed to have written the famous ballad, but the news report also noted that he was the nephew of David Graves George.

A *Danville Bee* article published on September 26, 1953, the fiftieth anniversary of the wreck, included a last paragraph that provides a suitable perspective to the story of Old 97:

The saga of Old Ninety-Seven has passed into history. There are no
longer any roundhouses where hostlers, the huggers, the blue-denimed
engineers and the sooty fireman can gather round to opinionate on what
happened to Joe Broady and his thunderhorse which he road into the
twilight of truth and legend.

What actually happened to train 97 that day will likely never be known. But we must see beyond the wreck itself. It portends the lessons of life that we all encounter and, for that reason alone, deserves to be memorialized. Robert Benson, opinion page editor for the *Danville Register and Bee*, wrote on September 26, 2003, the 100th anniversary of the wreck, "The wreck of Old 97 was much, much more than just another fatal train accident. It became an indelible blue collar tragedy—working men, behind a furious schedule, literally trapped on a fast track to a horrible death."

Then there is the comment by Johnny Cash in the DVD *Ridin' the Rails*. As the singer rehearsed America's railroad history, he reflected, "When I was a boy the trains ran passed my house and they carried with them the promise that somewhere down the track anything would be possible."

Perhaps both statements explain why the wreck of Old 97 lives on in story and song. It has become an epic tale about what's around the next curve, whether promise or pain. We have all faced trestles in our lives—or will—but we accept those challenges with the hope that we can make the grade and keep on rolling.

Joseph Broady would understand.

SELECTED BIBLIOGRAPHY

Only works of particular value to the wreck of Old 97, both story and song, are listed below. A number of other widely available works on railroading, steam engines, the history of the Old 97 wreck and the history of the ballad were also referenced in the manuscript but are not included here. Personal interview subjects are included in the acknowledgments.

BOOKS AND BOOKLETS

Adams, Charles Francis. *Railroad Accidents*. New York: G.F. Putnam's Sons, 1879.

Carneal, Raymond B., Jr. *The Wreck of No. 97*. Winter Park, FL: published by author, 1978.

Clemmer, Lloyd. *Wreck of Old 97*. West Palm Beach, FL: published by author, 1960.

Cohen, Norm. *Long Steel Rail: The Railroad in American Folksong*. Urbana: University of Illinois Press, 1981.

Conner, E.R., III. *On Time to Monroe: Legend and Lore of the Southern Railway Washington Division*. Berryville: Virginia Book Co., 1971.

————. *Railroading on the Washington Division*. Manassas, VA: REF Pub. Co., 1986.

Fox, Pat. *The Wreck of the Old 97*. Danville, VA: Fox Publications, 1969.

Gregory, G. Howard. *History of the Wreck of the Old 97*. Appomattox, VA: published by the author, 1992.

Kirkman, Marshall M. *The Science of Railways: Passengers, Baggage, and Express Mail Service*. Vol. 5. Chicago: The World Railway Publishing Co., 1904.

Lester, James Elisha. *My Most Unforgettable Experiences, Including the Wreck of Old 97*. Unpublished manuscript, March 3, 1967.

Popek, Diane. *Tracks Along the Staunton: A History of Leesville, Lynch Station, Hurt, and Altavista*. Altavista: Altavista Printing Co., 1984.

Prince, Richard. *Southern Railway System: Steam Locomotives and Boats*. Revised edition. Green River, WY: published by the author, 1970.

Robertson, James I. "The Wreck of Old 97." Unpublished copy. Danville, VA: Chamber of Commerce, 1955.

Shaw, Robert. *A History of Railroad Accidents, Safety Precautions, and Operating Procedures*. 2nd ed. N.p.: Vail-Ballou Press, 1978.

Striplin, E.F. *The Norfolk and Western: A History*. Revised edition. Forest, VA: Norfolk and Western Historical Society, 1997.

Watt, John C. *Car Builders Dictionary of American Practice. Series 1879–1916*. New York: Master Car Builders Association, 1895.

Webb, William. "Investigation into the Wreck of the Old 97." Unpublished copy. Danville, VA, 1998.

NEWSPAPER ARTICLES

Alexandria Gazette, September 28, 1903.

Caswell Messenger, March 8, 1995.

Commercial Appeal, January 12 and 19, 1976; September 13, 1976; September 15, 1958.

Danville Bee, September 28, 1903; September 26, 1953; September 27, 1963; September 1976.

Danville Register, October 30, 1977; December 1, 1986; September 1987; September 25, 1988.

Danville Register and Bee, November 18, 1991; August 30, 1992; November 6, 1994; September 26, 2003; September 27, 2003.

Danville Virginian, January 8, 1986; January 19, 1986.

Danville Weekender, September 27, 1980.

Evince, January 2003; September 2003.

Greensboro Daily News, January 9, 1938; September 22, 1982.

Greensboro News and Record, September 21, 2003.

Gretna-Hurt Gazette, September 27, 1974.
Honolulu Star-Bulletin, September 22, 1963.
Morganton News Herald, October 1, 1903.
New York Times, February 2, 1901; September 28, 1903.
Pittsylvanian, September 1968.
Raleigh News and Observer, September 29, 1903; December 10, 1978.
Richmond News Leader, September 28, 1903; September 29, 1903.
Richmond Times-Dispatch, October 16, 1938; June 6, 1953; September 27, 2003.
Roanoke Times and World News, September 27, 1987.
Rockingham Register, October 2, 1903.
Salisbury Post, April 7, 1954.
Virginia Star, August 10, 1933.
Washington Post, September 28, 1903.
Washington Star, November 5, 1967.
Winston-Salem Journal, April 5, 1992.

MAGAZINE ARTICLES

Hamilton, Lieutenant Commander Maxwell. "The Wreck of the Ol' 97." *Retired Officers Magazine* (May 1983).
Herbert, Hiram. "The Wreck of Old 97." *Saga* 13, no. 3 (December 1956).
McKinney, Robert. "The Wreck of Old 97: Who Drove that Train Anyway?" *Blue Ridge Country* 14, no. 5 (September/October 1991).
Robertson, James I. "The Wreck of Old 97." *Virginia Cavalcade* 8, no. 2 (Autumn 1958).

JOURNALS AND PAPERS

Cohen, Norm. "Robert W. Gordon and the second Wreck of 'Old 97.'" Reprint from *Journal of American Folklore* 87, no. 343 (January/March 1974).
David Graves George Papers, 1903, 1928–1966. Small Special Collections Library, University of Virginia.
Scott, Alfred P. "The Origins of a Modern Traditional Ballad: Wreck of the Old 97." Senior thesis, University of Virginia, 1965.
White, N.I. et al., eds. The Frank C. Brown Collection of North Carolina Folklore II and IV. Durham, NC, 1952–64.
"Wreck of Old 97." *Virginia–North Carolina Piedmont Genealogical Society Bulletin* 22, no. 3 (August 2000).

MAPS

Conner, E.R., III. *Washington Division Route*. Adapted from *Railroading on the Washington Division*, 1986.

Dabbs, Melissa, and Corey Furches. *Southern Railway Route through Danville, circa 1900*. Danville, VA: City of Danville GIS Department, 2010.

Insurance Maps of Danville, Virginia. New York: Sanborn Map Co., 1920.

Mainline Map: Monroe to Danville. Adapted from Wreck of Old 97. N.p.: Lloyd Clemmer, 1960.

Section Southern Railway: Still House Branch Trestle. Danville, VA: T.M. Bass, 1905.

Stillhouse Trestle, Then and Now. Danville: City of Danville, Virginia Engineering Department, n.d.

COURT RECORDS

Estate of Joseph A. Broady v. Southern Railway. Corporation Court files, 1905. Circuit Court Clerk's Office, Danville, VA.

Victor Talking Machine Company v. George. Federal Reporter, Series LXIX (April–May 1934).

———. Federal Reporter, Series CV (September–October 1937).

MISCELLANEOUS MATERIALS

Cohen, Bob. "Virginia Midland et al Ownership Genealogy." E-mail, 2010.

Cooper, Betty Clark Anderson. "Wreck of the Old 97." March 31, 2000.

Griffin, William E., Jr. "The Abandonment of the Lima Branch into Danville." Unpublished manuscript, n.d.

Lewey-Payne, Shirley. "Daughters in Search of Their Father." Ezfolk. com. http://www.ezfolk.com/bgbanjo/bgb-tabs/wreck97/wreckbio/wreckbio.html.

Oral Recordings on CD
  Interview with John Wiley by Lynwood Yarborough, n.d.
  Interview with Ruel Bullington by Clara Fountain, January 15, 1976.
  Yarborough, Lynwood. "History of the Wreck of Old 97," 1978.

Southern Railway Public Timetables, November 2, 1902.

Southern Railway Station Directory No. 5, July 1, 1912.

Southern Railway Train Order No. 217, September 27, 1903. Southern Railway files.

"Statement of Time Made by Joseph A. Broady, Engineer." Memorandum from Southern Railway Company, n.d.

Stephenson, David R. "Discussion of Tractive Effort and Horsepower." Unpublished manuscript, 2010.

————. "Statistical Charts Comparing Engine No. 1102 to Other Locomotives." Unpublished manuscript, 2010.

ABOUT THE AUTHOR

L arry Aaron is associate editor of *Evince* newsmagazine and a published historian from Danville, Virginia. He has received first-place awards for his writing from the Virginia Press Association and also edited the award-winning book *Danville in the Civil War* by Lawrence McFall. Among his published works are *Aaron Ancestors of Pittsylvania County, Virginia*, a genealogical study; *Keppy's War*, the memoirs of Captain John Kepchar in World War II; *The Race to the Dan*, a history of events in the southern campaign during the American Revolution; and *Pittsylvania County: A Brief History*, published by The History Press.

Visit us at
www.historypress.net